Modern Pathfinders of Christianity

Modern Pathfinders of Christianity

The Lives and Deeds of Seven Centuries of Christian Leaders

By

HENRY KALLOCH ROWE, Ph.D.

Professor of History and Social Science,
Newton Theological Institution

Essay Index Reprint Series

BOOKS FOR LIBRARIES PRESS

FREEPORT, NEW YORK

First Published 1928
Reprinted 1968

LIBRARY OF CONGRESS CATALOG CARD NUMBER:

68-16973

PRINTED IN THE UNITED STATES OF AMERICA

PREFACE

THE present revival of interest in biography warrants a new appraisal of the value of Christian biography as a means of religious education. Human lives are the best interpretation of the spirit of a period; it is the story of the life of Jesus rather than of His teachings that humanizes the Gospel. The history of the Church, similarly, may be studied through the leaders who animated the whole body of Christians.

Biography presents ideas directly, concretely, dramatically; it gives an opportunity to study the development of character, and the reasons for success or failure; it serves as a nucleus for the larger history of the time in which a man lived. By a study of successive leaders it is possible to have a connected story of all Christian progress.

All these are reasons why ministers and teachers of religion should make more frequent use of biography. In the pulpit or the prayer room, in adult and young people's classes in religious education, and in reading circles in the parish, it is practicable and stimulating to introduce the lives of men who have lived to good purpose in their period of history. This is the reason for this book.

H. K. R.

Newton Centre, Mass.

CONTENTS

I

BLAZING THE ANCIENT TRAIL

FOR nineteen hundred years the trail of Christian history has been winding its way over continents and seas from the ancient East to the farthest West. In the land of Palestine at the crossroads of ancient civilization the trail began. In tentative fashion it wound in and out among the villages of Galilee, as Jesus ministered to the soul-sick and physically ill. It meandered over the Samaritan hills and down the Jordan valley by different routes to Jerusalem. It led to Gethsemane and Calvary and Joseph's tomb in the garden, and there it seemed to lose itself in the gloaming.

The spirit of Jesus could not die. He had pointed out the path and pictured the goal at the end of the trail. He had explained the way of life and virtue, and had given the dynamic that set men on pilgrimage. After He had gone who first blazed the trail, others took up the torch. They carried it out into Syria, along the Roman roads of Asia Minor, and to the farther cities of the Roman Empire. Christian pathfinders went to Alexandria and explained the way of Jesus where Egyptians dwelt and Greeks thronged the streets and Hebrews plied their trade. They crossed the sea to Rome, and zigzagged to Spain and southern Gaul. They turned their ship's prow to Carthage on the North African coast, and there Latin Christianity

9

grew prominent. They followed east and west to the farthest limits of the Empire. Men of faith and courage and vision were they, commissioned by the living Christ to carry His name and teaching to the end of the world.

Many were the pathfinders of the ancient Church. They varied in personal ability and in the capacity to think deeply and to act vigorously. Some of them excelled, and moulded the thinking or directed the action of Christians over considerable areas of country. Like the potter at his wheel or the artist in his studio, they fashioned the plastic human stuff with which they worked. Christian groups had their problems of Christian conduct and organization as churches do now, but their leaders had to find their own way to a solution, instead of relying on methods sanctioned by centuries of tradition and past experience. They had to formulate their doctrinal waymarks. Men of Jewish stock evangelized in Jewry, but in the broader environment of the eastern Mediterranean Christianity must be interpreted by Gentiles. Men who had been timid in Greek modes of thought did most of the writing. Out of the harvest of apostolic letters and memoirs a selected sheaf of Christian literature was taken, by common consent of the churches, and it became a New Testament of the Founder of their faith and a guide for their spiritual pilgrimage. Within three centuries the religion of Jesus had won a victory over rival pagan religions and a pagan government jealous of its popularity and power.

Among the pioneers of ancient Christianity were

heads of prominent churches, such as Ignatius of Antioch, second century martyr for his faith, and Cyprian, bishop of Carthage, who fell victim to Roman persecution one hundred and fifty years later. Others were scholars, thinking through the intellectual problems that religion cannot escape, and writing or teaching for the instruction of those who had less time or ability to think. Such were Clement and Origen and Athanasius at Alexandria, and Tertullian and Augustine in the province of North Africa. Chrysostom was a silver-tongued preacher at Constantinople; Jerome made a Latin translation of the Bible that is still standard for the Roman Catholic Church; Benedict of Nursia organized the growing movement of monasticism.

While the Christian Church was taking form and gathering strength for its forward march, the Roman Empire was tottering slowly to its fall. In the East it was to last yet many centuries, but it no longer pushed out its frontiers among less civilized races. Churches in the East remained grouped around the leading centres, each independent of the others, but they lacked virility as well as unity and the spirit of pioneering was weak. The trail of future Christian progress was not to be blazed by eastern leaders.

In the West the destruction of imperial government under the blows of migrating Germans from the north made it possible for the masterful Roman bishops to strengthen their position of authoritative leadership. By degrees they became real rulers in civic affairs as well as over the religion of the people, and their ambition grew to enjoy such sovereignty as the ancient emperors had possessed. The path of spiritual progress became fainter as it passed into northern Europe in the Middle Ages. Mediæval missionaries went beyond the old frontier of the Rhine and the Danube. The road was policed by the clergy of the Catholic Church. Monks and friars and lordly bishops passed along the trail. Beside the road sprang up many a church and monastery, each with its priest or abbott and his monks. In the six centuries between 600 and 1200 the Roman Catholic Church came to control the trail with its ecclesiastical legions as completely as ever the ancient emperors with their armies.

The prominent names of the makers of the mediæval Church were Pope Gregory I, who gave renown to the papacy and who sent the first Roman Catholic missionaries to England; Boniface, preacher and organizer of the Christian Church in Germany and France; Pope Gregory VII, who achieved reforms in the churches and monasteries; Bernard of Clairvaux, monk and mystic, defender of the faith and of the papal prerogative; and Pope Innocent III, under whom the climax of power was reached.

The thirteenth century marks the culmination of the progress of the Roman Catholic Church. In Pope Innocent III the Church had a head whose will was obeyed in the palaces of kings as well as in the huts of peasants. Dictating political affairs in Germany, where kings had tried to restore the ancient dignity of the Roman Empire, taking national tribute from England, compelling a powerful French king to take back

his divorced wife, the Pope played the lord over the
most powerful countries of Europe.

The Catholic ecclesiastical system was characterized
by unity of organization and faith, by the authority
of the bishops, of whom the Roman Pope was chief,
and by certain sacraments administered by priests,
sacraments deemed essential to the salvation of the
multitudes for whom the Church was responsible.
Unity of organization had been secured by centralizing
power in the hands of men who were capable of guard-
ing the faith, administering discipline, and managing
ecclesiastical affairs efficiently.   Unity of faith was the
product of ecclesiastical synods and councils which
formulated creeds and insisted on conformity to those
norms.   The strength of the whole system rested on
the belief that the priests by withholding the sacraments could doom a man to eternal punishment.   Excommunication from the Church was the terror of the
sinner and the nonconformist.

At the same time that the Church was making con-
quest of the State, it was binding the human reason.
No one could think for himself, least of all modify his
religious opinions.   A few men tried.   Abelard, a
teacher at Paris, dared to appeal to reason as an arbiter
in theological questions.   It was a rash thing to do.
The dogmas of the Church had been fixed.   Unity and
authority must be maintained, and Abelard had to
make his peace with the Church.   It was not forbidden
to argue about how a particular doctrine could be
true, but it was not permitted to argue whether it was
true.   To find an intellectual proof for one's faith was

good mental exercise in a fenced corral, when the mind was not permitted free range, but the open fields looked desirable.

To make the Catholic position plain Thomas Aquinas, the most eminent theologian of the Middle Ages, set off sharply the fields of reason and of faith. In the one field men could discuss, in the other they must believe without question. In his *Summary of Theology* he outlined the position of the Catholic Church for all time. Fifty years ago the Pope at Rome declared that there was no reason to question the conclusions of Thomas Aquinas, and he should be accepted as a theological authority.

In spite of the apparent victory of the Roman Catholic Church, the thirteenth century was a time of unrest, of dissatisfaction with the intellectual and political situation. Under the spur of the Crusades, of changing conditions of social life in country and town, and of university study and discussion, the mind of man was awakening. The promise of a better day was on the horizon.

There was, first of all, a new national consciousness. For a long time the feudal régime in the different countries of Europe had broken them up into small districts, each semi-independent of any central government. England and France, Germany and Italy, were geographical designations rather than nations. It was partly this lack of national unity that made possible the rule of the Popes. But in the thirteenth century there was a growing appreciation of what the nation meant. The origin of the House of Commons in England was just ahead. The Third Estate of the commonalty was soon to be represented in the Parliament of France. There was to be a new national solidarity that would present a stern front against a foreign pope.

There was also a new social consciousness. In the mind of a peasant on a rural estate an ambition was beginning to stir that in time would make him a free man, and would drive him out into the world to make his fortune. He had been a serf too long. He became ambitious to be his own master. In the cities were opportunities for manufacturing and trade, out of which were to come modern capital and the arts of business.

There was, too, a new spirit in religion. Too long had the people looked to the priest for guidance and to the Church with her sacraments to make them right with God. But Waldensian preachers in southern France were pointing their audiences to the Bible instead of to the priests, and summoning them to win salvation for themselves instead of trusting them to the sacraments. This new evangel was an echo from the first Christian century, and it was to grow louder until it was heard through the length of the Rhine country and over into the valleys among the Italian hills. The lay evangelists appealed to the Pope for sanction of their preaching, but they were forbidden to preach except after Catholic ordination, and therefore they went out to organize their Waldensian groups independently. They were the first harbingers of a movement of protest against the old Church. The pathfinders of modern Christianity were on the way.

2

FRANCIS OF ASSISI

U P among the Umbrian hills is the Italian city of Assisi. Its brown stone houses climb the slopes that rise above the plain, and higher rise the Apennines which form the backbone of Italy. It was in the Italian peninsula that Benedict of Nursia drew up the rules for the monks of Europe. There was the capital of Christendom. It was appropriate that an Italian hill town should cradle a movement which was to mark a new departure for Catholicism, and to indicate an interest in two practices that are prominent in Protestantism, preaching and service. It was a movement that, like the Waldensian movement, had its springs in the Bible. It was promoted by evangelism. It gripped the common people. It was lay and democratic in its inception. But it remained Catholic, because its founder was able to secure the approval of the Pope. Like a statue half-chiselled from the marble, it was held in restraint by the old order of religion, but it was prophetic of new forces for a new world.

In the twelfth century the Italian cities were stirring centres of industry and trade. In Assisi lived Pietro Bernadone, a successful cloth merchant, with business connections in many places. In 1182 he became the proud father of a son whom his mother named John,

16

but when the father returned from a journey he preferred to call him Francis. He is known in history as Saint Francis of Assisi, and even the twentieth century remembers his anniversary and gives him its admiration.

The Italian cities were centres of an active social life as well as of trade. The boy grew up to enjoy the gaieties of his native city, and became a leader among the youth. He shared lavishly in the prosperity of the family, and seemed likely to enjoy a life of ease and pleasure. His happy life and good fortune were interrupted by a war that broke out between the two cities of Assisi and Perugia. Every Italian city was a law unto itself in those days, and local quarrels easily developed into interurban wars. Francis went to war as heedlessly as to a carnival, ready to lead in adventure and daring. But he found himself a prisoner shortly, and languished in confinement for a year. At the end of that time he fell dangerously ill. This made him feel that life was serious, and when he returned home he gave himself to prayer and almsgiving. He thought he could satisfy his conscience by putting on a beggar's clothes, and embracing a leper. He bowed humbly before God in the church. Frequently with a friend he visited a grotto in the country where he used to pray that God would show him His will. Gradually he recovered from the depression that had followed his illness, and he planned to resume the life of a soldier in behalf of his country against the foreign Germans. But in a dream he saw that the military career was not for him. He could serve God best by using spiritual weapons against invisible foes, as had his Master, Jesus Christ.

Filled with an inward joy that he knew what was his duty, he told his companions something of his purpose, but they did not understand him. He seemed like a youth in love, and they asked him if he was soon to marry. Yes, he said, to a lady of wealth and beauty such as the world never saw. The poet Dante celebrated his nuptials in these verses:

> " Still young, he for his lady's love forswore
> His father, for a bride whom none approves,
> But rather, as on Death, would close the door.
> In sight of all the heavenly court that moves
> Around the eternal Father, they were wed;
> And more from day to day increased their loves.
> She of her first love long bereft, had led
> A thousand years and yet a hundred more,
> By no man sought, life hard and sore bested.
>
> .   .   .   .
>
> But lest my hidden words the truth shall veil,
> Francis and Poverty these lovers were,
> Of whom I weave at too great length my tale."

Resolved to be poor, Francis began to give away his money. That did not take long in a land so full of beggars as Italy. When his money was gone he gave even the shirt off his back. Passing a church one day, he entered to pray, and it seemed to him that the Christ on the crucifix spoke to him and told him to carry out needed repairs on the building. He hastened to the priest and gave him money, and then he went home, helped himself to rich clothes in his father's warehouse, mounted his horse and rode to a neighbouring city, where he sold the cloth and even the horse. Returning to Assisi, he turned over the proceeds to the priest of the church.

When his father learned of this escapade, he was angry at such squandering of property, and punished his son by confining him at home. Hard-headed man of business that he was, he had no patience with the spendthrift intentions of his son. His mother gently reasoned with Francis to be more sensible, but it resulted only in an obstinate decision to renounce his family connections and go his own way. He surrendered all claims to an inheritance, refused even to take clothes from his father, and in the dress of a pilgrim he wandered forth, a knight errant of religion.

In the Middle Ages to be religious was to become a monk. In a monastery, removed from the temptations and distractions of the world, a man might hope to cultivate his soul by holy exercises so that he would obtain favour with God. The monk turned his back on all family and social responsibilities, and selfishly, though with many hardships, strove for his own salvation. Francis might have become a monk, but for his loving disposition. He possessed a quality, rare in those days, of a soul in love with the lowliest of God's creatures. He went out to minister to the needy by the hedges and the byways. He had loathed the sight of a leper, but, as he said, the Lord Himself did lead me among them and I had compassion upon them. In a little church called Saint Mary of the Angels he heard the priest read the commission of Jesus to His

disciples: Wherever ye go, preach, saying: The kingdom of God is at hand. Heal the sick, cleanse the
lepers, cast out devils. Freely ye have received, freely
give. Provide neither silver nor gold nor brass in your
purses, neither scrip, nor two coats, nor shoes, nor
staff, for the labourer is worthy of his meat. This message seemed to be meant for him, and he took it
literally. This was the dynamic that impelled him to
preaching and social service.

Such a method of being religious, so familiar in our
time, was not then customary. In the thirteenth century there were two kinds of people sharply marked
off from one another. The mass of men and women
made up the laity of the Catholic Church, but they
bothered themselves little about religion except by at-
tending church and sharing in the Mass, and in time of
need saying a prayer that they had learned to the
saints or the Virgin Mary. Religion was an affair of
tLe clergy, who claimed to be the medium of communication between man and God. It was this position of
privilege and power that made them able to control the
minds and conduct of the people. Every rural village
was the parish of a priest, and the parishes were
grouped into dioceses under the control of bishops.
The whole system headed up in the Pope at Rome.
Everybody was a Catholic parishioner under the
authority of the clergy.

Besides these were the members of monastic orders,
regularly of the order of Benedictines. Similar to the
monks in purpose and life were nuns, women who had
withdrawn from all relation to society, as had the men,

and were trying to find peace of mind and heart or refuge from the ills and wearing burdens of home or community life. Monks and nuns had become so numerous that mediæval society was deprived of many of its best people, a misfortune comparable to the loss to social progress that comes from the death of many of the most valuable citizens through modern war.

It is for these reasons that the decision of Francis to serve others rather than himself as an expression of a religious purpose was profoundly significant. Suppose others should follow his example and change the custom of centuries. And it was morally certain that the contagion of his example would seize others in such an age.

Francis went away from home clad in his gray-brown serge cloak tied about his waist with a piece of rope, and with his feet bare. He would work for his bread, if chance offered, but if not he would beg his way for Christ's sake. He attracted two followers who joined him in a hut which they made their home. Thither in the plain of the Rio Torto came others, beating a path to his door because of their admiration for him. There Francis had dreams of crowds coming from afar to learn the simple way of being Christians, and there he drew up simple directions for his followers, based on the Benedictine vows of poverty, chastity, and obedience. More important to Francis than any rule was the spirit of service that to him was essential to true religion, and he cared little for forms if the right spirit dominated his followers.

The nature of Francis was a simple one. Catching

the spirit of his Master, his one purpose was to serve his fellow men. He could not see why conduct should be hedged about with regulations. He did not desire to establish a new order. It was enough to take the words of Jesus as a guide, and live humbly and sincerely. But no movement succeeds without certain forms to give it character and substance. This explains the tendency towards organization of the Franciscan movement.

While yet in process the new enterprise was submitted to the Pope for his sanction. The story is that Francis and his companions came into the presence of Pope Innocent III as petioners for his favour. They were wayworn and unkempt, barefooted, and meanly clad in their gray gowns. Innocent was the autocrat of Catholic Europe, surrounded in his palace at Rome by every evidence of power and splendour. Why should such a pope give recognition to a poor company of laymen? It was not often that the papacy failed to make use of various agencies to accomplish its ends, finding a place for each new movement in its ecclesiastical system. But a new spirit of independence and free association was abroad, and it was becoming dangerous. It was appearing in the gilds of the cities, and in circles of religious reform springing up all over southern Europe. Of what use could such a band as these laymen be to the powerful Church of Rome? It is easy to imagine Pope Innocent shaking his head, supercilious, if not scornful, for he declined the request. But tradition says that Innocent had a dream picturing the rapid growth of the new order, and presently he gave his sanction to the popular preachers, but with the proviso that they must be ordained as priests. Lay movements were not wanted in the Catholic Church.

The approbation of the Pope made the Franciscans popular. On their return journey from Rome they were welcomed with pealing bells and people in procession; large gifts were made to the movement in spite of the wish of Francis that strict poverty should be the rule; and at Assisi the church of Saint Mary of the Angels was turned over to the company for its use. Wealth and honour were thrust upon the new order, with the same temptation to which so many of the monasteries had yielded to live in luxury and self-indulgence. But as yet the friars were true to their initial purpose. Francis was compelled to make a more elaborate code of rules, by which he hoped to secure obedience to the principles that he laid down for the mendicant movement. The organization was centralized by placing a superintendent over it, called the minister-general. Francis was the first to hold that office. The members of the order called one another brothers, hence the name friars.

To appreciate the work of the mendicant friars it is well to picture in imagination the life of the masses in mediæval Europe, and the laxness of the clergy. The squalid lanes and huts of the rural peasants, the offensive streets and wards of the growing cities, the refuse heaps outside the walls and the hovels where the lepers congregated—all these sent out their voiceless cry of spiritual hunger and physical wretchedness.

The priest offered the people the sacrament of the
Mass, but he did not preach repentance for the remission of sin.   He was more of a pagan priest than a
John the Baptist.   But the friars came into village or
city, gathered the people on the green or in the market-
place and announced the plain gospel of Jesus in their
own language, not in ecclesiastical Latin.

The Franciscans were the home missionaries of their
time.   They made their way over Italy, and across the
Alps to other parts of Europe.   Like the Salvation
Army they preached in the city streets, made their way
into the squalid quarters and ministered to the poor
and sick, and outside by the refuse heaps they were
merciful to the lepers.   They put up with the poorest
accommodations.   In Oxford, England, when they arrived, they were permitted to use a hall which served
as a schoolroom for boys, and during school hours they
had to shift for themselves in the cold.   Some of them
tried foreign missionary work.   Francis himself went
among the Moslems, but without success.   In later
centuries Franciscans were to accompany Spanish ex-
plorers to America, and to penetrate the vast area of
the southwestern part of the United States in missionary service to the Indians.

The Franciscans were mostly of the humble ranks
of society, unlike the monks who had come usually
from good families.   Few of them had an education at
first, and Francis did not value learning highly.   But
the Franciscan order became famous for its intellectual
achievements and its members filled high positions in
mediæval universities.

Such an object lesson of devotion as were Francis and his fellows could not fail to impress others. Soon a friend of Francis, a woman named Clare, became the head of an order of nuns, named after her Claresses, with rules similar to those of the men. Many persons whose responsibilities would not permit full observance of a mendicant life but whose spiritual purpose was the same, undertook to live lives of piety and service, and were bound together as a third group with the name of Tertiaries.

While Francis was gathering a group of like-minded followers, a Spaniard named Dominic, trained as a theologian by a ten years' course in a Spanish university, came into contact with the heresy of the Albigensians in southern France, and was moved so deeply by its prevalence that he resolved to devote his life to the suppression of heresy and the instruction of the people. Convinced that the parish priests were not capable of coping with the situation, he organized his order of black-gowned friars, the Dominicans, to preach and suppress heresy. He too received the sanction of the Pope, and after a little adopted the Franciscan vow of poverty.

Each order had its distinctive features. As a rule the Dominicans were the more aristocratic and better educated. They were known distinctively as preaching friars, and they became managers of the Catholic court of the Inquisition for the trial of heretics. Both orders were alike in the nobility of their initial purpose; both became corrupted by wealth and power. They became rivals in the faculties of the universities, where they gained a reputation as teachers of philosophy and theology. On the honour rolls of the friars are the names of Thomas Aquinas and Duns Scotus, Albertus Magnus and Alexander of Hales among the Schoolmen, Roger Bacon the pioneer scientist, Fra Angelico the artist, Savonarola the reformer, and even Martin Luther, the protagonist against the Catholic Church.

If the mendicant orders could have preserved the ideals of their founders and maintained the principles that animated them, the Church and society both might have benefited greatly from their existence, but it was not long before the simple life that Francis had introduced yielded to the ambition of other leaders than Francis, and wealth and power came to the orders. The secular clergy in charge of local parishes, whose more selfish lives were reproached by the devotion of the friars, rejoiced in the decline of mendicant virtue instead of helping to prevent it. The Franciscans divided into two parties, a majority favouring an easier life, the Spirituals striving to imitate Francis, but tending to become fanatical. The health of Francis broke down soon after he was forty years old, and he died in 1226, sad over the failure of his followers to keep the high standards that he had set.

As a man Francis deserves our admiration. In point of cleanliness, thrift, and education he leaves much to be desired, but in purity of purpose and absolute devotion to principle few could equal him. He was peculiar. He was fond of nature, delighting in the companionship of animals and birds. He dropped

behind his companions along the road and preached a
sermon to the birds on the need of gratitude to God.
He did other queer things. Perhaps his mind was not
perfectly balanced. But he loved God and his fellow
men. By that test he was Christlike, and that is the
one test that counts. If he could have multiplied
himself in his followers the social life of much of
Europe might have been improved greatly. He had
no conception of what modern science could do for
the material improvement of civilization. His principle of mendicancy is unsparingly condemned by
social scientists. But he had a spiritual principle that
the world sadly needs. For that Francis shines as
one of the beacon lights of religious history.

Francis was no Protestant. He had no quarrel with
the beliefs of the Church or its ecclesiastical practices.
But his guiding principle was so contrary to that of the
Catholic Church that his movement was an unsettling
influence, and is an evidence of a religious awakening
that was to bring far greater changes. The Franciscans were pioneers of religious reform.

The friars are reminders of the primitive Christians,
and of the Methodists and Salvationists of modern
times. All of them went about doing good, interested
in social as well as spiritual ministry, believing in the
principle of service and trying to find ways to apply
the principle. In that way as well as in their evangelical preaching they were distinctly modern. In the
mendicant movement the transition begins from the
old ecclesiastical system to the new and more vital
Christianity of the present day.

3

JOHN WYCLIF

IN their wanderings over Europe certain of the friars reached the English Channel, found their way across, and went to Oxford. Wherever they entered European towns the people welcomed their preaching in the streets, their homely phrases and their mother wit. They spoke in phrases that the people understood, and they were a delightful contrast to the lazy, ignorant priests. When they came to Oxford the Franciscans, true to their humble principles, made their dwellings in timber and mud huts in the low lands in the edge of town. They busied themselves in helping the sick and the lepers as well as in preaching, and they were admired for their self-forgetful service.

In Oxford they found a growing university. It had started when the thirst for learning brought swarms of youths from all over the country to drink in the lectures of teachers who had gathered the lore of the Continent. They formed groups of eager listeners by the wayside or in a dooryard. They crowded into small quarters indoors. They were a lawless crowd. They brawled with one another and with the townsmen. They looted houses of Jews, begged and stole from Christians on occasion and when the whim seized them they migrated to another student centre. In the thirteenth and fourteenth centuries Oxford gained a brilliant reputation with such famous exponents of science and philosophy as Roger Bacon, Duns Scotus, and William Occam. Friars became famous as teachers and made the University well-known for its loyalty to freedom of scientific inquiry and its championship of freedom from a papal overlordship of England, which had been claimed from the time of Innocent III.

It was into this atmosphere that John Wyclif when a youth came from his native Yorkshire about the middle of the fourteenth century. His own people of Yorkshire inherited an attitude that was not very cordial to the Pope. Many centuries earlier the Christian religion had been brought to the north of England by Irish missionaries who did not own allegiance to the Pope of Rome. It was only gradually that the sovereignty of the Pope over all the western Church came to be acknowledged. The Roman form of Christianity had been brought into southern England by missionaries sent by the Pope, but it was not for one hundred and fifty years after these missionaries had landed that the whole of England accepted the headship of Rome. Perhaps something of the early independence still remained.

At Oxford Wyclif was attracted by the insurgent spirit, and he won reputation as a scholar, but no one thought that he would become an even greater reformer than Occam. His spare form did not promise such sturdy independence as he exhibited later on. His reputation as a philosopher did not suggest his popularity as an evangelistic preacher. But he was

energetic, bold, and convinced of the need of reform
in Church, State, and society. When he became master
of Balliol College in Oxford University he was known
as the leading Schoolman of his time, and he became
recognized as a progressive thinker in politics, social
interests, and religion.

It is difficult to think of Oxford as harbouring ideas
that are revolutionary. The quiet reaches of the river,
the gray stone piles of the college quadrangles, the still
corridors of chapels and libraries, are eloquent of conservatism and peace. It is easy to think of young
Wyclif listening to lectures or poring over old parch-
ments. It is less easy to imagine him punting up the
Cherwell within the grounds of Magdalen College. It
is difficult to think of him as denouncing in his lecture
room the claims and practices of the Church, and
shocking even the most radical with his skeptical attitude towards the significance of the Mass.

Wyclif was sympathetic with the political tendencies
of his nation, which had been indicated by Magna
Carta, the beginning of the House of Commons, and
the royal declaration of the right of the nation to tax
the clergy of the Catholic Church. In spite of meagre
sources of information about his life, it is known that
Wyclif had very definite ideas about government. He
sympathized with the political principles of Marsiglio,
an Italian of Padua, which struck at the temporal
sovereignty of the Pope, and insisted on character as
the sole claim of the clergy to esteem. Wyclif declared the validity of these principles for Englishmen.
He wrote a tract on Dominion, in which he laid down

the principle that all the political rights of a sovereign depended on whether he met all his obligations to his subjects. On that moral ground he condemned the papal claim to the overlordship of England. He opposed payment of the annual tribute which had been paid from the time of King John. He favoured the demands for reform that Parliament was making, such as stopping the appointment of foreign priests to English parishes and the appeal of ecclesiastical court cases to the papal tribunal at Rome. He declared the king and Parliament supreme over churchmen.

It is unlikely that Wyclif realized how far he was moving from established standards, but in the contention that the control of conscience belongs only to worthy men was a seed of the Protestant Reformation. In the Catholic Church the primary factor in religion was not the character of the priest, but the regularity of the ceremony. The sacrament of the Mass was necessary for future salvation; it was much less important that the priest who celebrated the Mass should be a good man. But in Protestantism the quality of character was to receive recognition. Wyclif's principle was a prophecy of the later reform.

By 1374 Wyclif was a doctor of divinity and priest of the parish church at Lutterworth. He was still a Catholic. But unlike most Catholic priests he was not content to accept without question all the teachings and practices of the Church. He spoke out as a prophet, and he knew how to play upon the minds of those who listened to him. By his preaching he reached the people, as in the classroom of Balliol College he spoke to scholars. Wyclif was dissatisfied with the conduct of the monks and friars. As he saw them at Oxford they had degenerated from the earlier standards of their orders and were deserving of censure. He criticised the priests because they were ignorant, lazy, and often corrupt. He frowned upon their ambition for political favour. He, like Saint Francis, believed that poverty should be the lot of the clergy.

On technical rather than theological grounds Wyclif differed from the Catholic Church in his explanation of the sacrament of the Mass. The differences were a minor matter, but they involved the principle of Bible teaching as against the doctrine of an authoritative church. More than once the Church tried to bring him to trial; five times the Pope denounced him to the nation and demanded his punishment, but his powerful friends would not permit him to suffer harm. The papal thunder had less force when two popes vied with each other in the exercise of ecclesiastical authority, as was the case after the Great Schism in 1378. From that time Wyclif spoke of the pope as antichrist.

One man in particular defended Wyclif when the Catholic Church condemned him for his independent principles. That was John of Gaunt, a member of the royal family, and so a man of consequence in affairs. John of Gaunt was not a man of noble character, but his interests were hostile to those of the Pope, and his friendship was valuable for Wyclif. Wyclif's support was worth having for the Government also. He en-

joyed the favour of a royal chaplaincy and for a time
was on the Continent on political errands. His defense of the national position gave him a reputation
among patriots, and his career at Oxford for the years
that followed was a brilliant one. But it is Wyclif as
a prophet of reformed religion that is of greatest importance to a student of Christian history.

In time Wyclif turned from criticism to evangelism
and Bible translation. He knew how preachers of a
popular sort could influence the common people of
England, and like Jesus in Galilee he sent out poor
priests who were in harmony with his thinking to
preach a simple gospel that would be biblical and
appealing. These men went out over the countryside,
speaking their evangel as they had opportunity, talking
with the people, and indoctrinating them with the
ideas of Wyclif. They were ready to listen to such
novelties, for they were on the eve of their social revolt
against heavy taxation and other forms of oppression.
They knew some of the verses of John Langland, who
in " Piers the Plowman " had pictured the hard lot of
the peasants. It is likely that Wyclif's poor priests
added fuel to the conflagration that broke out in the
Peasants' Revolt.

If the teaching of the Church was not to be trusted,
and even the poor priests might err, where could one
go for instruction in the truth about religion? Wyclif
realized the need of such a source, and he found it
in the Bible. For the assistance it might render to
the evangelists and for the sake of the ignorant people
he undertook the translation of the Bible from the

Latin of the Vulgate into the English tongue. As in other countries so in England the mediæval Latin, the language of the Church and of literature, was being discarded for the vernacular in sermons and in lawyer's pleas, and English was taking form in the lines of Chaucer, the first of her great poets. Wyclif himself made the translation of the New Testament into vigorous, idiomatic English, and his friends aided in the production of the complete work. Wyclif's Bible was the pioneer among a number of translations that accompanied the Protestant movement in England. It did not go back of the Latin to the original Hebrew and Greek, but it was a model for later revisers and for other writers in the vernacular.

During Wyclif's lifetime came serious social disturbances. Normally the peasants worked stolidly on the landed estates of the gentry, and a middle class was coming to consciousness in the growing cities, but an abnormal condition had been produced by the Black Death, a visitation of the bubonic plague, which ravaged all Europe and forced certain social and economic changes. In some sections the population was reduced one-half. Not enough workers were left to maintain the agricultural industry. Scarcity of labour produced its usual effect in rising wages, which the landowners found it difficult to pay. It was hardly profitable to keep on with agriculture at a time when modern methods of increasing production had not yet come to the aid of the farmer. Many landowners let their cultivated acres lie untilled. There was only one other way out. The workers must be forced to work for lower wages. Only increased production could justify the high returns to labour, and that seemed impossible.

The determined effort to force the workers to yield to the will of the employers, coupled with heavy taxation by the Government, drove the peasants into revolt in 1381. The country was alarmed. Social revolution seemed imminent. The king met the assault with fair promises, which the peasants accepted at their face value, and the insurrection ended almost as soon as it had begun. No immediate gains were made by the workers, but within their lifetime most of the reforms that they had demanded were obtained. The significance of the uprising is the symptom of industrial unrest that appeared. England was not to continue under the feudal régime. It was on the way to becoming a real nation, with a recognition of the rights of all classes. Wyclif did not instigate the revolt, but his insurgency seemed to encourage it, some of his followers were among its leaders, and it lost him the support of the aristocracy.

The next year after the Peasants' Revolt Wyclif was condemned at a church synod held in London, but his popularity kept him from harm, and he continued to write and preach. In 1384 he died and was buried at Lutterworth. He had foiled his enemies while he lived, but thirty years later his opinions were condemned at the great Catholic council of Constance, and his body forbidden to lie in the consecrated ground of the churchyard. As a consequence his body was exhumed and burned, and the ashes were thrown into the

Avon River, to be carried to the sea and scattered world-wide, as his teachings had been.

The influence of Wyclif was especially powerful among the Lollards, as his followers were called. It was as if he offered to his fellow countrymen the Bible in one hand and evangelical preaching in the other. Preaching had not been characteristic of church services in the Middle Ages, and the direct address of the poor priests was the more effective. It was not unlike the effect on later England of the preaching of the Methodist itinerants who went around on preaching circuits. The people responded as they did to the preaching friars a century earlier. The evangelists were able to make a successful appeal because they sprang from the people and knew them. It was their custom to point to the Bible as the guide to practical religion, and Wyclif's Bible circulated widely, though it was handicapped by the necessity of making manuscript copies before the days of printing. Later on the Catholic Church tried to seize all copies of the Wyclif Bible, but they were hidden when possible by the people who prized them, and copies were in existence a hundred and fifty years later at the outbreak of the English Reformation.

Wyclif pronounced a great truth that had become overlooked by putting so much emphasis on the services of the Church in making a man right. Personal character had not been sufficiently stressed until Wyclif made it essential to religion. He believed that immorality broke that link that binds man to God which is essential to religion. He showed in himself qualities of moral greatness. He was true to his convictions, outspoken in his preaching, courageous in his attitude towards those who had the power to do him harm. He anticipated what others were to say more effectually about indulgences, pilgrimages, and other customs of the Church, and so was in truth a " morning star of the Reformation." England was not yet ready for profound religious changes, but Lollardy was a herald of Lutheranism.

The teachings of Wyclif made their way to the Continent. Jerome of Prague was a student at Oxford in the last years of the century, and he carried back to Bohemia the opinions of the English reformer. Bohemia had been always rather independent of Roman control, and the University of Prague was a centre of intellectual ferment. John Huss, for a time the head of the University and an evangelical preacher in his Bethlehem Chapel, like Wyclif in Oxford, received favourably the doctrines of Wyclif, and incorporated them into his teaching. He attacked the same abuses that Wyclif had denounced, and was widely influential among his people. A ban of excommunication from the Pope drove him into retirement, and he was condemned and burned as a heretic by the Council of Constance, but his countrymen rose against the German emperor who had failed to protect him according to his promise.

The movements of Wyclif and Huss were symptoms of the growing dissatisfaction with the Roman Catholic ecclesiastical system. It had grown from humble beginnings to a proud position of leadership in European affairs. It exercised social control through its clergy who were found in every trading centre and rural hamlet. But far too many of the clergy had low standards of attainment in education, morals, and religion. They could not make the people any better than they were themselves, and it was easy to make religious forms, like the Mass, a substitute for the religion of the heart. Tradition and the strength of inertia long kept the masses of the people loyal to the Church, but that loyalty would not last if once the people became convinced that the Bible was more to be trusted than the clergy, and if they learned that the essence of religion was the inner attitude of the soul rather than church or sacrament. It was this that made Wyclif and Huss dangerous, and made the Catholic Church oppose the Bible of Wyclif.

In increasing numbers here and there men and women were reading for themselves. They were getting together in prayer circles to talk and pray about the spiritual experiences that they were finding possible for themselves. Schools were being maintained for the education of young people so that they might be able to do their own thinking. A rebirth of human consciousness had come, a consciousness that there was value in the individual man and he was not merely a cog in a machine. Humanism was a new gospel in Italy, and beyond the Alps it blossomed into a new appreciation of what human beings might become through a spiritual religion. This was the Renaissance. When the Renaissance had freed the human mind, the Reformation was not far away. The Church had prepared the soil by its own failings; the Renaissance had sown the seed of intellectual insurgency; the Reformation was to be the harvest. Just when it would come could not be foreseen, but there was no question whether it would come. Cardinal Julian, writing to the Pope of conditions in Germany, said: " Human spirits are waiting for what is going to happen, and they seem bound to give birth soon to something tragic. The malice that they have against us is declaring itself; soon they will believe that they offer to God a pleasing sacrifice in maltreating or spoiling churchmen as a class hateful to men and to God, and plunged into the extremes of evil. . . . God takes away from us the vision of our perils, as He is wont to do with those whom He wishes to punish. The fire is kindled before us and we run away."

4

MARTIN LUTHER

NINETY-NINE years after the death of Wyclif a boy was born in Germany who was to convulse his country more than Wyclif had stirred England. Germany at that time was a loosely organized empire of almost independent states under the leadership of the Austrians. Its people had a reputation for piety. Most of them were unremitting in attention to the claims of the Church; here and there a few met for prayer and Bible study in groups of Brethren, as they called themselves, that they might learn the meaning of personal religion. The Renaissance had come to Germany, and with it a new interest in the Bible and in the individual. The time was ripe for a masterful leader, who would articulate the thought of those who were meditating upon religion.

In 1483 a boy was born in Saxony who was to become such a leader. Only a miner's lad, Martin Luther had few advantages, until he entered the University of Erfurt, but he was an eager student and gained a reputation for scholarship. Certain experiences that came into his life made him thoughtful about religion, and in those days to lead a religious life was to become a monk. Unexpectedly to his friends Luther left the University for the monastery, and for years he tried to find satisfaction of soul through ascetism and meritorious acts. The prime motive of the monk was to save his soul from a future of possible sin and suffering. Luther worked at it so hard that he became morbid, and nearly broke his physical constitution.

At that critical point in his life his superior, Staupitz, advised him to go to the Bible for spiritual comfort, and as Luther read he saw by degrees that it was not what a man might do so much as the way he might feel and think that was most important. It was his attitude towards God that counted most. If he would put his confidence in Christ instead of in his own good works to set him right with God, he might find peace. While he was in perplexity of mind, he was sent to Rome on an errand for the Augustinian order to which he belonged, and his experiences there strengthened his growing conviction that there was something radically wrong with an ecclesiastical system which was based on a theory of worthy acts and yet sometimes violated all the moral and social commandments.

While Luther was much tossed about in his mind, he was invited to teach in a new university at Wittenberg, not far from Erfurt. Staupitz had seen that it would do Luther good to get away from thoughts about himself, and the Elector Frederick, ruler of Saxony and founder of the University, was glad to get an instructor who would expect little pay. At first Luther taught philosophy, but later became professor of theology. Absorbed as he was in religious interests, he had studied theology and obtained the degree of doctor of divinity, which was regarded as evidence of fitness to teach. The more he taught the harder he studied,

and presently he was writing commentaries on books
of the Bible that were the basis of his system of
theology.

Luther might have come very slowly to the conviction that the teaching of the Catholic Church was
wrong, if he had not had his attention called to the
sacramental system of the Church by a sale of indulgences. It happened in the year 1517 that a young
German named Albert had been appointed by the Pope
to be Archbishop of Mainz. It was an office of prominence, and it was expected that the archbishop would
pay to the Pope a large sum for the pallium, a woolen
scarf which was the badge of his office. The Pope
wanted money especially for the building of Saint
Peter's cathedral. The only way by which Albert
could raise the sum needed was by borrowing from the
banking firm of the Fuggers in the city of Augsburg.
The archbishop eventually could secure enough to pay
his debt to the bankers from the German people, if
he should organize a sale of indulgences, or pardons,
granted by the Church to free the people from the
penalty of their sins. The interested parties agreed
upon this scheme of finance, and the sale of indulgences was started with the expectation that the religious German folk would hasten to purchase the stock
in the kingdom of heaven.

The sale was going well when John Tetzel, the
agent, came to the Saxon border and sold his pardons.
This attracted the attention of Luther. Convinced
that such a method of obtaining forgiveness of sin and
escape from its consequences was wrong, Luther re-

solved to bring the matter for debate to the scholars of Germany, and he wrote out certain statements which he proposed to defend and posted them on the bulletin board of the University. These were the famous Ninety-five Theses of Reformation history. An enterprising printer translated them into German and published them broadcast, and Luther awoke one morning to find himself famous. He had made himself the champion of a popular dissatisfaction that had been growing steadily as the people contrasted the teaching of Scripture with the words and the acts of the Catholic clergy. The sale of indulgences became unpopular, and the Catholic authorities were much disturbed.

At Rome the matter was not regarded so seriously. The Pope thought it was only a local squabble, but the order of Augustinian friars to which he belonged was told to silence him. A convention of Augustinians was held therefore at Heidelberg, to which Luther went, and there he found not a few of his fellow members sympathetic with his attitude, and Luther went back home cheered over his prospects.

The next attempt of the Catholic Church to discipline this insurgent son was to issue a summons to go to Rome for trial, and an indictment was issued against him to make clear his offense. Luther replied to the indictment and through his own prince, Elector Frederick of Saxony, he was able to get his trial transferred to the German city of Augsburg on the ground of his ill health. Thither Cajetan, the Pope's representative, journeyed from Rome and Luther from Wit-

tenberg. They met at the home of the Fuggers, who
entertained the distinguished Cajetan. Cajetan announced to Luther the condemnation of the Church, but
Luther insisted on debating the questions at issue until
Cajetan was glad to bring the interview to an end, and
Luther slipped away to Wittenberg before he should
be arrested.

Luther drew the attention of John Eck, a champion
of Catholicism, and Eck wrote against him in a document called " Obelisks." Luther replied in his bold
fashion in certain " Asterisks." Presently Eck drew
Luther into a long and formal discussion held at Leip-
zig in Saxony, where Eck compelled Luther to admit
that he agreed in his position with John Huss, whom
the Catholic Church had condemned for heresy at the
Council of Constance a hundred years earlier. Meantime the Pope had sent a messenger into Saxony to try
persuasive methods with Luther.

None of these methods won over Luther or in-
timidated him. He remained at Wittenberg teaching his
classes and writing fast and furiously on the practical
issues of his contentions. He was sure by this time
that he was correct in his ideas, and when he was once
convinced he would not surrender to any other man's
opinions, not even to the judgment of the whole
Church. He strongly suspected that the Pope was antichrist, spoken of in the book of Revelation. He appealed to the German nobility to defend his movement,
and to free Germany from bondage to the Roman
Church. He condemned the sacramental system of the
Church. He declared that the individual had a right to

judge for himself between the old Catholic scheme of salvation and the new Protestant way, which was that of the Bible. The Catholic Church had done what it could to save the situation, but it was compelled to issue a public condemnation, and Luther was excommunicated formally and given over to the State for punishment. It remained to be seen whether Germany would take upon itself that responsibility.

The year before the formal condemnation of Luther a new German emperor had been elected. The choice had fallen upon the young king of Spain, Charles, who thus became the Emperor Charles V when only nineteen years of age. He was loyal to the Church, like other Spaniards, and he summoned the princes of Germany, both lay and ecclesiastical, to meet in imperial diet in the city of Worms. The great assembly came together in 1521. Luther was summoned before its bar by a papal herald, and he rode across country in a carriage prepared for him. He expected that he was going to his death, but when his friends tried to persuade him not to go, he declared that he would go to Worms though as many devils might be there as there were tiles on the housetops.

It was a brilliant assembly made up of the dignitaries of State and Church, and at first Luther was overawed. When asked what he had to say for himself, he asked for more time. But the next morning he had recovered his courage, and when the demand was made that he recant all that he had said he refused, and taking his position on what the Bible taught he declared: " Here I stand. I can do no other." The

Council eventually condemned him, but before that happened Luther had started for home. On the way as he was riding through the Thuringian forest he was seized and hurried away from his friends and his enemies, only a few of those who were faithful to him knowing the place of his retirement. For a year he remained there in safety, throwing off his monk's gown, letting his beard grow, and spending his leisure time in undertaking the translation of the Bible into a new German edition.

Luther's defiance of the ecclesiastical authority of Rome won him the admiration of princes. His championship of a simpler, less expensive religion based on the Bible gave him the support of the people. His Bible translation was a model of modern German. He helped the people by preparing guide-books for worship and preaching, and he stimulated their religious feeling by means of German hymns. God was to him a mighty fortress, and his great hymn of faith sang itself into the hearts of the fatherland.

While Luther was in the Wartburg castle it was a grave question whether the movement that he had started would succeed. There was a general feeling that the Catholic Church needed to be reformed from top to bottom, but there was no agreement as to how it should be done. The Pope and his court at Rome had no wish to be reformed, as appeared at the three councils that had been called in the fifteenth century with the express purpose of reform. The head of the Church enjoyed his authority. The clergy would have liked greater freedom from overhead control, and some of them wanted permission to marry, though that was contrary to the rule of the Church in the West. It was a well-known fact that greed and licentiousness were common faults in the Church though by no means universal. The clergy expected to be paid for every religious act, church taxes were heavy, and the sale of relics and indulgences drew much money from the pockets of the faithful. In return for their hard-earned money people got religious instruction, for many of the priests were ignorant.

Two questions were acute. Should not more radical changes be made than Luther had made thus far? And, Should not reforms extend from the Church to the social order? Not a few persons answered both questions in the affirmative.

Luther's own disposition was to make haste slowly. He was naturally conservative. It had taken him a long time to reach the point where he must break with the Catholic Church. He cherished the hope that the break would not be permanent. He hesitated to make changes in the organization of the churches that had thrown off their Catholic allegiance. He still favoured a theory of the Lord's Supper that was essentially Catholic. But while he was in retirement the radical element at Wittenberg, led by Carlstadt, a professor in the University, pushed through further changes. They altered the mode of observing the Supper. Private masses were abolished. The occupants of the monasteries were urged to leave the cloister and marry, and the monasteries were to be broken up. The people were to make their own interpretations of the Bible, and turn the old schools into shops. Students began to go home from the University and the faculty to break up. It appeared as if all stability in the reform movement would be ended.

When Luther heard of these doings he decided to return to Wittenberg, though it was dangerous for him to leave his retreat. He appeared in his old pulpit on Sunday and on other days, and with tact and patience won the people back to his policy of moderation. He did not check all progress, but he was cautious. In time he, a monk, married a nun. But that was not yet. And Luther believed that the government should decide just how far the changes should go.

The question of social reform was as serious as the religious. For centuries Germany had been organized on the feudal basis, an organization of society which permitted the control of the common folk by the class of the landed nobles. The people were mostly serfs with many exacting duties of service to the lord, and with no freedom to leave their homes, or to gain any advantages. They lived under feudal oppression. For more than a century before Luther growing dissatisfaction had provoked local uprisings, when a castle or a monastery was burned and a few persons were killed. Nothing permanent came from such insurgency, but it was a symptom of unrest. When the Reformation swept Germany, it seemed to certain leaders among the working people that it was a proper time to strike for freedom from their overlords. If the Germans were to get rid of papal overlordship, why should they not also free themselves from feudal oppression? Luther's strong language in favour of the principle of emancipation encouraged them.

Two years after Luther's return to Wittenberg the Peasants' War broke out. The revolutionists drew up Twelve Articles in which they expressed their demands. These included the right to choose their own pastors, and to enjoy ancient communal privileges of which they had been deprived, such as pasturing their cattle on the common feeding ground. They also refused to remain serfs any longer. Impetuously they attacked their oppressors, and before the nobles could rally their forces scores of castles had been sacked. Luther was alarmed at the outbreak and tried to make peace, but failed. When the peasants refused to take his advice, he urged on the lords to punish the insurgents without mercy. Luther was theoretically in favour of the principle of emancipation from oppression of every sort, but when the principle was applied to concrete events he shrank from the consequences. In this case he realized that the revolt would discredit his whole movement, and he thought the religious reformation far more important than the social.

As soon as the landholders could get their forces together they were able to check the uprising, and they slaughtered the poor peasants. No good result came from the revolt, and it had the unfortunate consequence of making Luther distrustful of the ability of the modern man to use his own judgment in religion. From that time it was certain that the German Reformation would cease to be independent and that its direction would be with the governments of the various states.

During all this time it was quite uncertain how the religious problem would be solved. For several years Charles V was too busy with the concerns of his wide realm to give attention to the revolt from the Catholic Church. Five years after the Diet of Worms another diet met at Speyer, and there the enforcement of the former edict was left to the several princes of the different states. But three years later at a second diet in the same place it was decided to enforce the edict. Then it was that a protest was drawn up and signed by certain of the princes and free cities claiming the right of the Lutherans to have their own religion. It was this protest of 1529 that gave the name Protestants to the followers of Luther, a name that was extended later to all those who rejected the Catholic faith.

The next year the Protestants presented their Augsburg Confession to the Emperor that he might know the principles for which they stood. A year later they organized a league for defense against their enemies. Charles V was too busy to give them much attention, and the Lutheran movement spread. Political rivalries became involved; some fighting took place; there was some shifting of control back and forth between Protestants and Catholics. In 1555 peace was arranged at Augsburg, which recognized the right of the princes to choose for their people between Lutheranism and Catholicism. If any persons were not pleased with the choice, they had the privilege of migrating elsewhere, but the principle of toleration was not accepted for any.

Among those who were rejecting Catholicism were

a number of rural peasants and miners and some artisans of the cities, especially in southern and eastern Germany, who interpreted the Bible more literally than Luther, and who organized a movement of their own. They were called popularly Anabaptists, because they rebaptized those who joined them in the belief that any baptism before the exercise of an intelligent faith and personal consecration was invalid. The Anabaptists were not liked by the Government, because they claimed that government and religion should be separate, and that they should not take office, carry arms, or make an oath. Some of them believed in the near approach of the day when Christ should return to earth, and there were certain of them who were disposed to use force to get Germany ready for that day. In the town of Munster in western Germany a few leaders of that sort set up a short-lived millennial kingdom amid social and moral chaos. This gave all the Anabaptists a bad reputation, though nine-tenths of them were guilty of no other offense than an attempt to practise religion in their own way. Both Lutherans and Catholics were so intolerant of the Anabaptists that their movement was crushed, and few remained to maintain their principles, except in the Netherlands where they were known as Mennonites.

Luther lived twenty-five years after he was condemned at the Diet of Worms. He busied himself with writing and teaching and preaching. He built into permanence the structure of reform that he had fought for so bravely. He arranged for the oversight of the churches, wrote catechisms for the instruction of

the young and homilies for the use of preachers. He
made a home for himself where he lived happily with
wife and children. He died in 1546 in the village of
Eisleben where he had been born, but his mature
life was spent at Wittenberg.

Luther was the pioneer of the Reformation that
swept northern Europe in the sixteenth century. He
deserves the credit due to the pioneer. He did not
carry the Reformation through to completion. In
many respects Lutheranism retained the complexion of
the religion that it inherited. But success was possible
only to a moderate revolution. And Luther paved the
way for others who should take the torch and lead the
way to further progress.

5

JOHN CALVIN

THE location of Germany in the central part of Europe made it natural that the Lutheran movement should radiate in all directions. But western Europe was to get its inspiration from another leader. While Luther was feeling his way to a firm footing in his religious thinking, John Calvin was born at Noyon in France in 1509. France was a Catholic country, but a few persons were inclined towards Protestantism. Calvin was to feel the impress of those liberal Catholics, and to become even more influential than they were in spreading the newer religious ideas.

Calvin's father wished to train him for the law, and he was educated for that purpose at Paris and elsewhere; but he preferred to transfer his interest to literature, and contemplated a literary career. He published an essay on Seneca, the old Roman, as an earnest of what he might do. But when he was about twenty-four years old he had a conscious change of purpose, and ceased to be a loyal Catholic. It seemed to him that he was willing to be a passive instrument in God's hands for anything that He might wish him to do. This experience led Calvin to emphasize the importance of the divine will in his theological thinking.

To be a Protestant in France was to incur the oppo-

sition of the Catholic Church authorities and of the
government which was in sympathy with the Church.
Calvin's active connections with the few Protestants in
Paris compelled him to go into hiding. His inclination to study made him use the time available, and he
worked on a volume of theological principles which he
was able to publish at Basle in 1536. This became
famous as the *Institutes of the Christian Religion*,
and passed through several editions. His purpose, as
he expressed it, was " to furnish a kind of rudiments,
by which those who feel some interest in religion might
be trained to true godliness." He believed that there
were many of the French who were longing for a true
understanding of the way to God. In his preface to
the book the author instructs the king of France in
the Protestant doctrine, hoping to make him more
kindly towards the reformers. The book and its preface gave Calvin a reputation as a Protestant leader
before he was thirty.

Calvin could not settle down to a steady occupation
in France because it was unsafe there for a heretic.
He spent some time on a visit to Italy, until he just
escaped arrest and trial before the Catholic court of
the Inquisition. During a lull in French hostility he
returned to France to settle his business affairs, and
resolved to make his home in Strassburg which already
had accepted the Reformation. To reach the city it
was necessary to make a detour, and on his way he
stopped at Geneva for a night's lodging.

While Calvin had been getting his education a reform movement had started in German Switzerland at

Zurich. In that city a reformed priest named Zwingli persuaded the city authorities to abolish the Mass and Catholic practices, and to refuse to permit the sale of indulgences. Zwingli agreed with Luther in most matters, but not in the principle of fighting with weapons for his principles. Zurich was opposed by certain Catholic cantons of Switzerland, and Zwingli was killed at the battle of Cappel in 1531. But his reform spread to the neighbouring districts of Berne and Basle and their dependent villages. William Farel, a French evangelist, toured those regions and came to Geneva, which was on the border of France. The people of that city were dissatisfied with their local government, which was controlled by the Catholic bishop of the city, and under the spur of the reform movement they revolted. Thus the scene was laid for John Calvin. There by the blue waters of Lake Geneva in western Switzerland was to be performed the second great drama of the Reformation.

Geneva was a junction point for highways that ran south to the Mediterranean, east into Switzerland, and along the north shore of the lake into Germany. Merchants and travellers had brought the Renaissance from Italy, and might easily disseminate opinions current in the city. The people were gay and pleasure-loving, feeling the stir of the currents of life that flowed through the town. Farel had been preaching to them, but he was not able to organize effectively a local reformation of religion. When he heard that Calvin was stopping over at the inn, he hurried to call upon him, for Calvin's reputation as the author of the

Institutes had gone before him, and Farel believed that Calvin was the man of the hour for Geneva. In conversation with Calvin, Farel declared forcefully that it was Calvin's duty to remain in the city and complete the revolution there. Calvin preferred the quiet life of a student at Strassburg, but he bowed to what seemed to him the will of God and decided to remain.

The people of Geneva had not become indoctrinated with a consistent system of Protestant principles. Who could teach them better than the author of the Institutes? The people were fond of gaiety and needed moral discipline. Who could train them to sobriety better than this man who in all things was submissive to the will of God? The people had chosen to govern themselves. Who could educate them to democracy better than the son of French universities?

Calvin was a stranger in Geneva, and his pale and studious looks did not recommend him as a man of force and action. He gained distinction in a religious debate in the neighbouring city of Lausanne, and at a conference in Berne he pleaded for a union of the Protestant churches. In Geneva he was appointed to be professor in sacred learning to the church in that city, while Farel remained pastor. As teacher Calvin lectured daily in Saint Peter's Church on the letters of Paul, and he soon gained a wide hearing. It was customary to have a sort of open forum once a week in the church, at which the people asked questions which the minister answered. Much confusion of thought was present, and the instruction of such a man as Calvin was needed.

In articles for the regulation of the Church Calvin proposed four reforms which he thought should be attempted. These were with reference to the celebration of the Lord's Supper, the use of psalms sung in church worship, the religious instruction of children, and marriage. His wish was to persuade the people to take religion seriously. He thought it best that the Supper should be celebrated no oftener than once a month in the three churches of the city where there was regular preaching. In order to prevent unworthy persons from participating in the ordinance Calvin proposed a board of censorship of morals which should have the power to cut off a person from his church connection, and further he suggested making a religious census of the city to find out how many could be depended on to carry out his reforms.

Calvin favoured the innovation of introducing congregational singing of psalms into the church service, and the training of a junior choir to carry the singing until the congregation had become familiar with the practice. For the instruction of the children in the rudiments of the faith a catechism was prepared, which contained a confession of faith to which all the citizens of Geneva must subscribe or suffer banishment. Because of the confusion about marriage customs, regulations were prepared for that important ceremony.

The moral censorship of Calvin was not so revolutionary as it has seemed to those who are unfamiliar with contemporary customs. It was an age when municipalities regulated details of conduct, of dress, and of ceremony. But there was a strong company of the younger folk in Geneva who did not like the rigorous attitude of this foreigner. They determined that they would banish him instead of accepting banishment for themselves, and before Calvin had fairly launched his program of reforms both he and Farel found themselves exiles from the city. They tried to enlist both Berne and Zurich in their behalf, but they were unsuccessful. Calvin went to reside at Strassburg, where he had intended to settle a few years earlier.

At Geneva Calvin had preached and exercised political leadership. In Strassburg he resumed his functions as a teacher and preacher. He was paid a small salary, but was compelled to eke out his living by taking boarders. It was during this that Calvin married a French widow, who made him a sympathetic wife and provided him with the comforts of a home of his own. He acted as pastor over a church of French refugees. His Strassburg experience made Calvin more competent to carry out his later responsibilities when he should return to Geneva.

At Geneva his friends regained control within three years, the city found that it could not get along without Calvin, and he returned on his own terms. During the years that followed he was compelled to fight for his principles, and he could not always get what he wanted, but to a remarkable degree he was able to dominate the situation. He was strengthened by the immigration of numbers of French Protestants who found homes in the city, and the last ten years of his life were relatively peaceful. He was intolerant to-

wards those who disagreed with him, and the worst
side of his character appears in his quarrel with Servetus. Servetus was a Spanish physician, who made
valuable discoveries in medicine, but he was well
known as a heretic in regard to the doctrine of the
person of Christ. An unbeliever in Christ's divinity,
he did not hesitate to declare his antitrinitarian beliefs, and when he ventured to go to Geneva and by
that act challenge Calvin to arrest him, he was seized
and presently put to death.

It was Calvin's ambition to make Geneva a beacon
light to the new Europe. He put his abounding
energies at work to produce a system of control that
would insure the success of his principles. If those
principles were to triumph, he must solve three problems, those of theology, discipline, and education.

The sovereignty of God was the central principle of
Calvinism. Other doctrines conventional to Protestantism completed his system. Calvin himself preached
and taught theology. He was assisted by other ministers who preached to the several congregations in the
city. He wrote commentaries on different parts of the
Bible in an attempt to interpret them to his people.
He was never very sturdy physically, but his indomi-
table spirit kept him at work until his death at the age
of fifty-five. The theology that he inculcated was in
substance that of Augustine, the great Latin father of
North Africa. There was the same emphasis on the
helplessness of man and the predestinating will of
God. Both thought that sin had so tainted human
nature that salvation was impossible without the grace

of God. Calvin found a place for man's faith as essential to bring one into union with Christ. In that he was in sympathy with Luther. But even faith was the gift of God. He did not, like Augustine, make the Church the necessary channel of divine grace. As a Protestant Calvin thought of the Church as the organized body of believers in Jesus, and the Lord's Supper celebrated by the Church as kindling spiritual life in the participant, but not as the Mass, the one essential means of salvation.

But to Calvin it was not enough to think correctly. One must live worthily. In stressing Christian conduct Calvin parted from Luther, who feared to emphasize the importance of works as obscuring his central doctrine of justification by faith. Every true Calvinist made character the object of his constant endeavour, and was always watchful against temptation to sin. Puritanism was cradled at Geneva, and Puritanism is the expression of the conviction that life is a serious responsibility with eternal life as the stake.

To reinforce the urge of righteousness Calvin introduced his disciplinary system. This included first a committee on morals made up of the ministers of Geneva and twelve others. This was called the consistory. It had power to exercise discipline over individuals to the extent of excluding them from church membership. The lives of the laity as well as of the clergy were carefully regulated. The way they dressed and the way they acted exposed them to criticism. All must conduct themselves soberly and with moderation, living in the fear of God and of the city authorities. The civil government was expected to carry out the decisions of the church authorities, using its powers of last resort to enforce church penalties.

The Church was officered by pastors, teachers, elders, and deacons. Each had his special function. Pastors preached and administered the ordinances of baptism and the Lord's Supper. Teachers interpreted Scripture and defended the faith. Elders were agents of discipline, sitting in consistory. Deacons had charge of poor relief. The election of church officers was rather complicated, with safeguards against the choice of unworthy men.

From the beginning Calvin had seen the need of a system of popular education. He did not lose his interest in it, and before his death he had crowned it with a university, which became the training school for Calvinist leaders in western Europe. The system of lower schools was regulated carefully by rules that Calvin urged upon the city council. He was concerned particularly with the religious education of the young people, and revised the catechism that they might be well-grounded in the basic principles of the faith. In theological instruction the city became renowned. Students from all over western Europe thronged the Academy and there obtained the theology that they disseminated everywhere. Large numbers of refugees came from France to Geneva, and many of them were attracted by the opportunities for higher education. Calvin improved every opportunity to get a hearing for the best scholars of the day whom he drew to Geneva when he could.

Geneva was a magnet to draw people to Calvin, and out of Geneva went an energy that acted upon neighbouring countries. France was the first to feel profoundly the influence of her expatriated son. Calvin was deeply interested in the welfare of his native France. He trained pastors for the native Protestant churches. In the last decade of his life more than one hundred such men left Geneva for France. Before the middle of the century more than twenty provinces had been evangelized, including more than thirty of the leading cities. In 1559, the year of the founding of the Academy at Geneva, a national synod of Reformed, that is, Calvinistic churches was organized, and from that time Protestantism grew. It appealed successfully to the higher classes of the population. Nobles and even royalty found division of opinion over religion. Acute feeling developed. By and by civil war broke out between Catholics and Protestants. In 1572 occurred the frightful massacre of Saint Bartholomew, in which thousands of Protestants lost their lives. Afterward the Huguenots, as the French Protestants were called, were granted toleration by the Edict of Nantes, but that favour was withdrawn subsequently, and Huguenots fled in large numbers to England and even America. In the end Protestantism found itself almost crushed out, and the Catholic Church has remained the prevailing institution of religion in France.

Down the Rhine valley and into the Netherlands Calvinism spread and became the approved form of Protestantism, though Lutheran influences had been felt earlier. The Dutch had to win their independence from Spain before they could be sure of toleration for Protestants, but a war for freedom was fought through successfully. Not all Protestants in the Netherlands agreed regarding matters of doctrine, but at the famous Synod of Dort, meeting in 1618, the Armenians with their more moderate ideas were condemned, and the Calvinistic church system, presbyterian in form, and holding to the strictest ideas of Calvin and his Genevan successor Beza, were approved. The Netherlands became a place of refuge for persecuted Protestant sectarians from England, like the Pilgrim Fathers.

In one other country Calvinism was established as the ecclesiastical system of the nation. This was Scotland. The leader of the Scotch Reformation was John Knox. For a time he was on the Continent, because it was unsafe for him to stay in Scotland. For a time he was minister to an English congregation in Frankfort in Germany, but he liked best to be in Geneva, for he believed fully in Calvin and his ideas. He preached to English refugees in Geneva in a hall opposite Saint Peter's Church where Calvin was minister. When the opportunity came he returned to Scotland, and in 1560 he was instrumental in giving to the newly organized Scottish Protestant Church a Genevan disciplinary system, a catechism and confession of faith, and an order of worship. From Saint Giles's Church in Edinburgh he sent his voice into all Scotland, and even Mary, Queen of Scots, in Holyrood Palace in the same city had to listen to his denunciations of her conduct.

Presbyterianism of the Genevan sort never gained permanent strength in England as in Scotland or Holland, but Calvin's influence had much to do with the Puritan movement in the Church of England, and the independent English-speaking churches, Congregational and Baptist, accepted the Calvinistic theology.

Calvin's place in history is assured. He was a man with the capacity of a statesman, able to affect the course of events in several countries, formulating a theology that has long maintained its ascendancy in more than one Protestant denomination, loving truth and sturdily defending what he thought to be truth, intolerant towards others after the fashion of his day, but conscientious in seeking their good. He made Geneva the capital of the Reformed faith. Not a pioneer like Luther, he enlarged greatly the scope of the Reformation. In the long history of the Christian Church his name fills a conspicuous place, because his influence has extended world-wide through the missionary efforts of Calvinistic denominations. He perpetuated the hold of Pauline and Augustinian doctrines on the minds of modern Christians. When he died the Pope of Rome is said to have remarked: " The strength of that heretic consisted in this, that money never had the slightest charm for him. If I had such servants, my dominions would extend from sea to sea."

6

ROBERT BROWNE

A THIRD ecclesiastical revolt from Rome was staged in England. The spirit of nationalism that was stirring in the time of Wyclif united the people after the War of the Roses. A spirit of religious insurgency resulted from the unconventional thinking of Wyclif, Luther, and such scholars as Erasmus and John Colet of Oxford.

While Luther was meditating upon the novel idea of salvation through personal faith rather than works of righteousness and churchly intercession, and while Calvin was an infant in a French cradle, Henry VIII became king of England. His father had consolidated the kingdom, made his Tudor dynasty secure upon the throne, accumulated a fortune, and paved the way for a successful reign for his son. The youthful prince was handsome and popular, sympathetic with the new learning of the Renaissance, and ready to do his best for England. He married for his queen Catherine of Aragon, a fortunate alliance for England from a political point of view, because Spain was then the leading power of Europe, while England was by no means her equal in wealth or extent of power.

Henry proved a masterful king, and as the years of his reign advanced he became so autocratic that he could not endure any obstruction to his will. His passions were strong and he lacked self-control. It was one of his ambitions to leave a son to reign after him, but after twenty years of wedded life only one sickly daughter survived among several children. His wife was much older than himself, and when he became infatuated with Anne Boleyn, a maid-of-honour of the queen, he wished to divorce Catherine and marry the young girl. He was ready to move heaven and earth to accomplish his purpose, but he could not move the pope, whose consent to the divorce was necessary, according to the rule of the Roman Catholic Church.

After some delay the king cut the knot that bound him, asserted the independence of the nation and its Church from Rome, and browbeat Parliament into declaring him Supreme Head of the Church in England. This meant, not that the Church in England ceased to be Catholic, but that it was no longer subject to the Pope of Rome. In effect the Church in England was now a national Catholic Church. The king was disposed to make certain reforms in religion, but he was conservatively minded and while he lived the Church did not become really Protestant. But he had taken the first step in revolt.

With the accession of the boy-king, Edward VI, the real ruler in religious matters was Thomas Cranmer. He was sympathetic with the Lutheran movement on the Continent, and within a short time he was revising the religious forms to make them Protestant. Forty-two articles of faith were adopted as the national confession of its Protestant belief, and a revised English prayer-book was provided for guidance in the matter of worship. These religious changes were made on national authority. Most of the people were willing to follow the leadership of their superiors, and cared little for theology or formal differences between Catholic and Protestant.

After a reign of six years Edward died, and his older sister, Mary, the daughter of the divorced queen mother Catherine of Aragon, succeeded him. She was the first queen of England to reign in her own right. She was loyal to the Catholic faith in which she had been reared. She reversed the action of Cranmer and his sympathizers, restored Catholicism, and even acknowledged again the ecclesiastical authority of the Pope of Rome. Most of her subjects accepted her decision without regret for they were still Catholic at heart, but she persecuted those who persisted in their Protestantism, including Cranmer, who was burned at the stake in Oxford. Some persons fled for refuge to the Continent.

Five years of religious tyranny during Mary's reign made the Protestants sigh with relief when news of her death came in 1558. Her half sister Elizabeth succeeded her. She decided in favour of Protestantism as the national religion, and insisted on uniformity in faith and practice, as her predecessors had done. Her long reign of forty-five years made the choice permanent. England had followed the example set on the Continent, and had aligned herself with those who insisted on national independence in religion as in politics.

But the changes that were made did not go far enough to satisfy certain Englishmen. Throughout

Elizabeth's reign there was a growing party of discontent. The more progressive partisans of Protestantism had exiled themselves on the Continent during the preceding reign, some of them at Geneva. There they came under the influence of Calvin, and his personality and ideas affected them so completely that they absorbed the spirit of Puritanism that he had set up in Geneva. They were made the more restless because such a reformed church as they desired had been secured in Scotland by John Knox, who was pastor of the English for a time at Geneva.

In the succeeding reign of James I Puritanism became a party label in political as well as ecclesiastical affairs, and civil war with Puritan victory followed in the next reign of Charles I. The term Puritan did not always mean the same thing. As a political name it indicated a wish to limit the king's absolutism. As an ecclesiastical designation it meant a party inside the Church of England which rather disliked episcopacy, though many Puritans were willing to keep the bishops, if necessary. The Puritans opposed certain Catholic survivals in the services of worship and in the marriage ceremony. The more thoroughgoing Puritans were sympathetic with the Genevan discipline and the presbyterian system of church courts. They believed that life was a serious probation, that conduct should be sober, and that failure to maintain high moral standards should be penalized adequately.

No movement of progress can go so far as Puritanism went without throwing off certain by-products of a radical sort. In England certain persons who became convinced that they could not reform the established Church according to their own ideas quietly withdrew from attendance upon the regular services of worship, gathered by themselves for the observance of religion, and even organized small churches on an independent basis. These independent groups increased in number about the turn of the century, and early in the reign of James I a number of them were to be found in exile in the Netherlands. Among these was a separatist congregation from eastern England, shepherded by Robert Browne.

Browne was born about 1550 into an honourable family of eastern England, and was graduated from the University of Cambridge. It appears that he accepted the insurgent ideas when ecclesiastical matters were being threshed out at the University. It was an exciting time at Cambridge, for Thomas Cartwright, the champion of presbyterian principles, was trying to hold his professorship there against the pronounced hostility of Whitgift, the archbishop of Canterbury. After a post-graduate period of teaching Browne studied theology privately with an Anglican rector of Puritan principles, and he expressed these ideas in sermons of his own to congregations that were disposed to listen to him. About the year 1580 Browne had progressed in his insurgency to the point where he was ready to separate from the national Church, and he began to denounce the Church of England as unreformed and unregenerate. He was particularly impatient with the whole episcopal system, because the bishops stood in the way of the reforms that he deemed so necessary. Presently the bishops forbade his preaching.

At this point Browne left Cambridge where he had been living, and went to Norwich in the county of Norfolk. There a number of Separatists were to be found already, and there he had a friend, Robert Harrison, who helped to fix Browne's ideas. Within a few months a local church was formed on the basis of congregational democracy, independent of any control by bishop or king, restricted to such persons as could give evidence of truly Christian character and purpose. In those days of intolerance for any who would not conform to the conventional ecclesiastical order it was to be expected that any such venture would be molested. The church authorities interfered and most of the small bodies of independents concluded that they must give up either religious convictions or their native land. They chose exile and removed to Middleburg in the Netherlands in 1581. A similar group from London went to Amsterdam about the same time, and somewhat later the Pilgrims went from Scrooby to Amsterdam, and from there a few of them found their homes in Leyden. These were the beginnings of Congregationalism.

Robert Browne was an impulsive man. He could not wait for the slow-moving Puritans who were reluctant to leave the Church of their fathers. To stir them to action like his own he wrote a tract on *Reformation without Tarrying for Any*. It is in this pamphlet and a companion tract on the *Life and Manners of all True Christians* that the historian

finds the key to the principles of Congregationalism.
Basic in his mind was the qualification of Christian
character as prerequisite to church membership.
Browne knew that religion did not thrive in an all-
inclusive church like the national Church of England,
which made no distinction between those who were
really Christian and those who were not. The Congregational churches therefore had a limited con-
stituency. In order to bring those who were qualified
into a church organization, a covenant must be adopted
as a bond among them and with Christ. The covenant
bond included children of members, who were to be
baptized and regarded as potential members of the
church.

An important feature was the congregational basis
of control, which disregarded all outside authority.
Christ was the head of the Church, and no bishop or
presbytery could assume the right to interfere. This
was a new departure in polity, more radical than the
presbyterian organization of Geneva or Scotland. But
perhaps the most revolutionary principle was the
democratic nature of local government. Not only was
every church free from outside control, but its members had an equal voice in choosing a pastor, managing
local affairs, and exercising discipline. Its officers
were about as among the presbyterians, but no
oligarchy ruled through kirk session or presbytery.

Two other ideas were in process of emergence, but
they were less well-developed. One was that a Congregational church should feel a sense of friendly concern for the welfare of other churches, an idea which

after a long time was to produce associations of churches; the other was that civil officers have no right to interfere in religion. Browne had seen how unfortunate such molestation was; he knew that politics and religion did not mix well. But in this tendency Browne was out of sympathy with his age, and the separation of Church and State failed of recognition as a congregational principle where it had its greatest opportunity in the Massachusetts colony.

Much as a liberty-loving man may admire the principles and the courage of Robert Browne, he loses confidence in him as a leader. A spirit of faction grew in the little church at Middleburg, and Browne showed himself unable to harmonize the factions. Before long he left the Continent with a few of his followers and went to Scotland, but the Presbyterian system there agreed with him even less than did his mother Anglican Church. Before long he was back in England, presently teaching school for an occupation, but he had a strong friend in Lord Burleigh, and probably through his influence he became Episcopal rector of a small parish church. There he remained, as in a quiet harbour after a storm, for a period of approximately forty years, while Puritanism was maturing in Church and State, and both Puritans and Separatists were finding their way oversea to America.

The movement towards independency in religion did not fail through the defection of Robert Browne. It naturally developed a spirit of individualism. Freedom from external authority tended to an emphasis upon individual rights and the assertion of individual opinion. Small as they were, the early Congregational churches were torn by internal dissension, and they were often unfriendly to one another. They tended to split up over minor differences, such as the baptism of their children or the exercise of adult discipline.

The most prominent of the early Congregational groups was a London organization which came into existence late in the sixteenth century. It had educated leaders in Henry Barrowe and John Greenwood, but both suffered for their faith. It was Barrowe's idea that the management of affairs in the local church should be in the control of the officers, not of all the members. This theory was of course less democratic than that of Browne, less truly Congregational. It was held by some persons, who were called Barrowists in distinction from the Brownists, followers of Robert Browne. Persecution of the London church was severe.

After the death of Barrowe and Greenwood, while other leaders were held in prison, many of the members made their way to Amsterdam. Eventually all arrived there, but the same spirit of faction which had disturbed Browne's congregation at Middleburg seized upon this Ancient Exiled Church at Amsterdam. The members were so insistent upon discipline for the slightest offenses and so constant in their mutual censorship that tempers slipped and sympathies awoke for accuser or accused, and turmoil soon increased. The wife of the pastor, Francis Johnson, was blamed by her brother-in-law for the fashion of her dress. This was sufficient to cause an uproar in the church.

Confusion and conflict increased with the advent of John Smyth and a congregation of Independents from Gainsboro in England. John Smyth was a Cambridge graduate with erratic tendencies. Like Browne he was brought up an Anglican, but he was convinced of Separatism and gathered a congregation of like-minded people at Gainsboro early in the seventeenth century. Drawing upon themselves the active hostility of the authorities, they, too, had to go into exile in the Netherlands. While the Ancient Church from London was afflicted with internal bickerings, Smyth quarrelled with it over nice questions of Bible translation and the use of psalm singing in worship. Never long contented with his position, Smyth became dissatisfied soon with his baptism. Probably he had been affected by the ideas of the Mennonites, the Dutch Anabaptists. He went so far as to rebaptize himself and his followers. But again he was dissatisfied, and before he had made other affiliation he died. These experiences weakened the Church. Others who had followed Smyth to his Baptist principles and practices returned to England and established the first Baptist church on the soil of England in 1611.

From the same neighbourhood in England which sent forth Smyth's Second Exiled Church in Amsterdam sprang the Pilgrim Church of Leyden and Plymouth. In the border district between Yorkshire and Lincolnshire were farming districts whose inhabitants had Gainsboro for their trading centre. Some of these rural people joined the group of Congregationalists who met in the town under the leadership of Smyth.

The most conspicuous of these persons was William Brewster, the postmaster on the high road in the hamlet of Scrooby. In the large manor-house which he occupied it became practicable to hold religious meetings, and after the coming of John Robinson it seemed safer and more convenient for the Scrooby company to separate from the Gainsboro company and to have Robinson for its preacher.

John Robinson was a native of the region, a graduate of Cambridge University, and for a time like Smyth a minister of the Church of England. He tended towards Puritanism and even Separatism, and when he came to Gainsboro he was a real accession to the Congregationalists. The humble congregation at Scrooby was soon beset by the hostility of the civil authorities, for the government of James I was determined to nip religious independency in the bud wherever it appeared. They tried to get away to the Continent but were hindered, and it was only after a good deal of hardship that they succeeded in finding their way to Amsterdam, a third company of English exiles in that city with independent convictions. They soon found the associations with the earlier congregations of refugees unpleasant, for they were not of a pugnacious spirit, and they chose a more agreeable place of residence in Leyden.

In the Dutch cities the English exiles were compelled to make a living as best they could. Ainsworth, the teacher of the Ancient Exiled Church in Amsterdam, found employment as a porter in a bookstore. The Pilgrims, accustomed to out-of-door occupations, did not take kindly to the city trades, but they made the best of the circumstances and gained the respect of the Dutch.   Brewster went into the printing business, Robinson was in close and pleasant relation with the University of Leyden, which was located only a short distance across a canal from the house where Robinson lived and gathered his people for religious services.

As time passed the Pilgrims found that their children were growing up like the Dutch, and were in danger of drifting away from their English connections and ideas.   Then, too, poverty continued to grind the exiles.   It was stimulating to them to see how a colony of Englishmen had established themselves at Jamestown in Virginia, and they reached a decision to emigrate from Holland to a point on the Atlantic coast of America where they could be free to practise their Congregationalism, and still be Englishmen on English soil.   It was a momentous decision for a small, impecunious company like the Pilgrims, but they were undaunted by danger and strong in their faith in God. They made the best business terms they could with those who agreed to finance them, and as many of them as could sailed in the *Mayflower* for America.

The story of their settlement at Plymouth is well known.   The hardships that they endured at first would have discouraged less hardy folk to the point of abandonment of the enterprise.   Disappointment in not having their pastor Robinson with them was keen. But they hung on when the day was darkest, welcomed friends who came later, and got on their feet economically. Plymouth became the centre of a colony that was never large or exceedingly prosperous, a colony that by and by lost its identity when it was merged with Massachusetts Bay. But the Pilgrims transmitted to the New World the Congregationalism that Robert Browne had fathered, influenced the Puritans about Boston to accept Congregationalist principles for the organization of their first church at Salem, and impregnated the soil of New England with the seeds of democracy and religious freedom. To achieve that was to be great. The importance of the Pilgrims was quite out of proportion to their numbers or their standing. They were a tiny group of middle class Englishmen on a waste of uninhabited shore, but the founding of Plymouth in 1620 was one of the landmarks in the history of human progress.

The movement of religious progress, so stimulated by the work of Wyclif and Luther and Calvin, had made its way into England, had percolated through the conventional mind of the Anglican to the heart and brain of the Independent, and in form of Congregationalism had crossed the ocean to a new continent. Robert Browne was the man who gave voice to the principles that were latent, and is called rightly the father of Congregationalism. But he went back into the Anglican fold. Henry Barrowe was faithful to his convictions until his execution, but he leaned towards Presbyterianism. John Smyth fostered the Congregational enterprise, but he was too individualistic and his restless mind carried him on to Baptist convictions. John Robinson is the best known of the

leaders, and he remained faithful to his church connections until his death.   Through their combined efforts they contributed to the strength and future freedom of American religion.

Robinson added to Congregationalism a progressive
principle, when he preached to the Pilgrims leaving for
America that more light should yet break forth from
God's holy Word.   True to that progressive principle,
modern Congregationalists have been leaders in the interpretation of Scripture and in the adaptation of
religion to current life.

7

ROGER WILLIAMS

WHILE the early Congregationalists were seceding in small groups from their ancestral church in England, the bulk of the Puritans remained in the established body hoping that further reforms would come in time. The Puritan was not altogether a man of religion. Often he was a man of affairs in politics or business. Certain men who had landed estates found that their incomes were less than were required for the proper standards of family life. Some of them were in trade on a considerable scale. For one reason or another not a few of them saw an opportunity to improve their fortunes or to obtain greater religious satisfaction by colonial settlement in America. Undoubtedly the flavour of adventure gave added attraction to the thought of emigration.

The result of all these causes was a large migration of Puritans during the reign of Charles I before the Civil War broke out. Many of the emigrants sailed to the shores of New England and made settlements in or near Boston Harbour. As each village in Old England had its parish church, so each settlement constructed its meeting-house, and within a few years the colonial legislature of Massachusetts passed a law that no one should live more than half a mile from the meeting-house, both for spiritual influences and for safety.

New England colonial life became village life, in which
the Church figured prominently.

In the first settlement made at Salem the basis of
church membership was the same as in the Church of
England. All estimable citizens were expected to belong to the church, and it was anticipated that epis-
copally ordained ministers would come out from England to meet the needs of such colonial churches. But
more mature consideration made it seem highly desirable that church membership should be limited to
those in sympathy with Congregational principles.
The conversion of Puritans still in the established
Church of England to separatists organized independently on the model of the Plymouth church may
have been due in part to the freedom from Anglican
influence, but it was specifically aided by conversations
between Salem leaders and Dr. Samuel Fuller of Plymouth, who visited Salem in time of severe sickness
in the northern colony. The Congregationalists at
Salem reorganized the church, limited membership to
those who could show spiritual qualifications, adopted
a covenant, and ordained their own pastor and teacher,
and the church was welcomed into Congregationalism
by representatives from Plymouth.

The influence of Salem was so strongly felt in other
communities that one after another Congregational
church was organized, until the whole colony became
Congregational in manner of church organization.
This was not pleasing, of course, to all. Certain persons, like John and Samuel Browne at Salem, disliked
the abandonment of the Episcopal prayer-book and the

reordination of ministers, but the authorities sent them back to England. Most of the Congregationalists maintained the fiction that they were still in the Church of England. But there were zealots on the other side who thought some of the churches too conservative. Such a man was Roger Williams, who declined an invitation to supply the Boston church, because it was not fully separated from the Church of England.

Roger Williams is another of the interesting characters produced by the English Reformation. Like other Separatist leaders he was a product of the University of Cambridge in England, probably a native of London. He adopted separatist opinions while a private chaplain on an estate in Essex County, and emigrated to America because he was out of sympathy with the Anglican Establishment. Williams was a gifted personality, capable of making fast friends, but unfortunately just as likely to provoke other persons to enmity by his outspoken remarks. When he was honoured by the invitation to be minister to the Boston church he met it with a rebuff, presuming to criticise the church for its failure to become thoroughly separatist, a failure that was mended soon afterward. The Salem church which was foremost in its separatism, found him acceptable for a teacher, in those days a copastor, and would have welcomed him had it not been for a protest from six of the prominent Boston men. The consequence was that Williams removed to Plymouth, where he found more congenial people than in the Bay colony. For two years he served as teacher of that church, and studied the language of the neigh-

bouring Indians. His acquaintance with the aborig-
ines was to serve him well later on.

Williams was liked at Plymouth until he began to
utter his own peculiar opinions, and then he found it
expedient to return to Salem. The Plymouth people
were more tolerant of differences than in the Bay
colony, but they expected a reasonable degree of con-
ventionality of opinion. He shortly became pastor of
the Salem church. Ministers of the Congregational
sort were too few to provide all the churches with
pastors and teachers, and Williams had more than one
opportunity to make himself acceptable in pulpit and
parish. But he could not stultify his conscience by
keeping quiet when he felt it his duty to criticise. In
his frank criticism he struck at the very roots of
colonial life regardless of the consequences, and at a
critical time in the fortunes of the colony.

It is not likely that the political and ecclesiastical
authorities in England would have permitted the establishment of Congregationalism in New England if
they had not been absorbed by other matters at home.
The one means of salvation to the dissenters in America
was to escape the notice of the king and his officials.
Any man who disturbed the peace of the colony was
especially dangerous because of the circumstances of
the time. Yet Roger Williams took that particular
time to utter his strictures upon the Bay colony. He
thought it wrong for the king to appropriate the lands
of the Indians and for the colonists to live under the
royal charter. He spoke of the king in the harshest
terms, and proposed to write him a letter in criticism

of his course of conduct. It is not strange that the
Boston Puritans were scandalized and fearful of the
consequences.

Not content with such political insurgency, Williams
freely criticised the Church of England and those who
kept any relation to it, and he kept away from all but
Separatists. This was often disagreeable to others.
He was peculiar also in opposing the practice of taking an oath or joining in worship unless a man was a
true Christian. He insisted that magistrates had no
right to interfere with any man's religion, a principle
of religious freedom that was shocking to most people
and governments. But it was Williams's acceptance
of the pastorate of the Salem church that particularly
vexed the men of Boston who so disliked him. He
proved a thorn in the side of the colony within a few
miles only of the chief town. The colonial legislature,
the Salem church, and the troublesome minister were
soon at odds, and before the end of the next year the
decision was reached that the colony must get rid of
so annoying a citizen. The authorities did not act
hastily, and because Williams was taken ill they permitted him to remain through the winter if he would
keep from criticism of the colony. When he disobeyed,
they planned to ship him to England, but he escaped
into the woods.

It was at that time that Roger Williams reaped the
reward of his interest in the Indians and their language.
He did not enjoy crowding into their filthy quarters in
the depth of winter, but for three months he was compelled to accept their hospitality, thankful that he lived

and was still in America. Eventually he settled at
Providence at the head of Narragansett Bay, where he
bought land of the Indians. Although he was out of
reach of the Massachusetts government, John Cotton,
minister at Boston, wrote a long letter to Williams, in
which he tried to make him see the error of his ways,
but this only provoked in rejoinder the defensive
volume of a thousand pages entitled *The Bloody
Tenent of Persecution*. In this deliverance he set
forth his own opinions in full.

Thus far we have made the acquaintance of Roger
Williams, the critic of the Bay colony. In that rôle
he has not appeared to advantage. Sympathy is rather
with the colony in its efforts to keep itself secure. But
as founder of a colony on a new principle of justice
and freedom he assumes a different character. It was
a rash experiment to admit into the colony of Providence men of all sorts and convictions and to try to
weld them into a body politic that would be progressive and yet stable. The principles of the separation
of the Church from the state, of the distinction between
a comprehensive state Church and a company of Christian believers, and of full religious liberty, were new to
the world. Continental Anabaptists had stood for
them, but had succumbed to persecution. Robert
Browne and John Robinson had had glimpses of such
great truths and had championed separatism of church
organization. But to found a colony like Providence
on such ideas in the seventeenth century was to court
almost certain disaster. Yet none were molested, even
Spanish Jews and the erratic Quakers from England.

Roger Williams enjoyed the advantage of having the loyal friendship of the Indians, and of a number of friends who followed him to Narragansett Bay. But news of a colony with unrestricted admission for any one who wished to come attracted all kinds of persons, and made it more difficult to maintain peace and good order. Still Williams clung to his principle of freedom, and the colony worked out its salvation from anarchy. Early in its history the colonists agreed to maintain the public good in civil things, leaving religion unmolested. It was natural that Massachusetts should like little the establishment of a colony so near by on such dangerous principles, and the hostility of the Bay was shown in a number of ways. At length in 1643, when Massachusetts, Plymouth, Connecticut, and New Haven, formed a political federation for protection against the Indians, the Providence colonists feared that they might lose their independence. Williams had given Massachusetts kindly warning against an attack from the Pequots, but in spite of that Providence was not recognized. It seemed advisable that the small Narragansett colony should acquire standing for its own safety. Roger Williams went to England. He was fortunate in arriving at a time when the Puritans were breaking the power of the absolutist king, and he was able to obtain from Parliament a patent securing to the Narragansett settlers their existence and their rights.

The parliamentary document provided for a union with Providence of certain other settlements that had been made farther down the bay. Among the settlers were Anne Hutchinson and her family from Boston. She, like Williams, had been banished because she was too outspoken in her criticism of a certain element in authority. These settlers were in harmony with the spirit of liberty that animated Williams, and they organized their government on that principle. A charter for the colony was secured on the king's authority in 1663.

For a considerable time the population of Providence was small, not more than a few families. Most if not all those who had come from Salem were Congregationalists. Williams was the only ordained minister. No attempt was made to construct a church building for many years; the people met for worship in private houses. Three years after he had left Massachusetts the restless mind of Roger Williams came to question his baptism as an infant in an Anglican church. There were English Baptists at that time who denied the right of a minister to baptize infants who could not be conscious of any personal experience of religion. Whether or not there were individual Baptists in the Providence colony who may have influenced Williams in the matter is not clear, but the result of his reasoning was that a certain Ezekiel Holliman of his company rebaptized Williams, and then Williams baptized those who were willing to join him. This action resulted in the organization of a Baptist church in Providence in 1639, which as far as is known was the first Baptist church in the United States.

About the same time Baptists organized a church in Newport, with John Clarke as pastor. Clarke was a physician who had come to Boston with the intention of practising medicine there, but the disturbances over Mrs. Hutchinson made him prefer to go elsewhere. On a visit to Williams at Providence he decided to settle on Rhode Island down the bay, and there he became the preacher for a small settlement. He too was converted to Baptist principles and became the pastor of a Baptist church in Newport.

Both in Providence and Newport differences of opinion arose as to certain religious practices. At that time there were some Baptists who thought it was as necessary that a minister should lay his hands on the head of a candidate for church membership as that he should baptize him. The ceremony was regarded as essential by those who were called Six Principle Baptists. This principle vexed most of the Baptist churches in Rhode Island during the years that followed. As for Roger Williams he became dissatisfied after a few months with the manner of his baptism. He felt as if the irregular way in which he had been baptized by one who had no authority handed down by clerical succession was unwise, if not wrong. The result of this questioning was the withdrawal of Williams after a few months from fellowship with the rest of the Providence church. Such questions as these, based on individual interpretations of the Bible, caused heart-searchings in persons of sensitive conscience; they seemed not so much matters of form as evidences of faithful obedience to divine commands. Small details were magnified in an attempt to get at the exact will and purpose of God.

From that time Roger Williams became known as a Seeker, like John Smyth after he had broken connection with his Amsterdam flock. He continued to reside on his farm near Providence, and more than once showed himself a useful member of the colony. More than once he used his influence to maintain peace between the Indians and the increasing number of settlers in eastern New England. The Indians trusted him and were always friendly to him personally. He realized the responsibility of giving them the Christian message. On his voyage to England in 1643, a slow progress in those days, he employed his time in writing out the information that he had gathered about the Indians, their language and customs. The book was published in London with the title: " A Key into the Language of America; or An Help to the Language of the Natives in that part of America called New England. Together with brief Observation of the Customs, Manners, and Worships, etc., of the aforesaid Natives, in Peace and War, in Life and Death. On all which are added Spiritual Observations, General and Particular, by the Author."

In order to mend his fortunes after his rather expensive voyage to England, Williams established a trading post down the bay. There he received furs from the natives in exchange for supplies which he furnished them, and from which he could ship to and receive goods from England. Meantime he carried on his farm and participated in the responsibilities of colonial life. He was friendly and hospitable to both white men and Indians, welcoming even Massachusetts men on occasion. He kept an Indian servant to shoot game for him. He treated the Indians when they were sick, and cured his son of epilepsy by the use of tobacco as a remedy. He had long kept a close friendship with Governor Winthrop of Massachusetts in spite of their differences of opinion, and it was Winthrop who advised Williams to steer his winter course as an exile to Narragansett Bay. This friendship was never broken through the long years of their lives. In a similar friendship Williams maintained a close relation with Canonicus, chief of the Narragansett Indians. When Canonicus died, he asked that his body might be wrapped in a garment that he had received as a present from Williams.

In the fifties Roger Williams was made colonial president, though he would have preferred the less responsible life of a farmer. Public affairs were managed best when his hand was at the helm. He was able to prevent an Indian war which threatened. He restricted the sale of liquor to the Indians. He had to suppress elements of discord as best he could. Throughout his life he was always a public-spirited citizen.

Roger Williams lived until after King Philip's War, which so harassed the outlying settlements of New England. The colony of Rhode Island opposed the war and attempted to mediate between the Wampanoags, of whom Philip was chief, and the colony of Massachusetts, but without success. Even Williams himself was unable to make peace, and the Narragansetts joined the war. Some of the settlements were attacked, and in spite of Quaker traditions of peace the colony had to defend itself. Providence was burned partially, but the colony survived the struggle for the mastery of New England, and peace returned.

In 1683 Roger Williams died. As a legacy to his fellow-citizens he left, as he said, but " one motion and petition, which I earnestly pray the town to lay to heart, as ever they look for a blessing from God on the town, on your families, your corn and cattle, and your children after you, it is this, that after you have got over the black brook of soul bondage yourselves, you tear not down the bridge after you by leaving no small pittance for distressed souls that may come after you."

The principle of liberty in religion was adopted by William Penn in his Quaker colony of Pennsylvania, and ultimately by the whole United States in the days of its constitution making. Only slowly did the principles of justice and equality among religious sects spread in Massachusetts, but in the nineteenth century all barriers to liberty and equality were broken down. The seed that was sown by Roger Williams has borne a rich harvest both in America and in foreign lands. Baptist churches multiplied in the later colonial period, and took their place with Congregationalists and Presbyterians in perpetuating the sectarian differences that had arisen in the Old World.

8

GEORGE FOX

AT a time when others were emphasizing the importance of forms of worship, ordinances, and the government of churches, it was natural that some persons should react against such externals in religion and put stress on a man's inner experience. If the essence of religion is spiritual, why bother overmuch with sacraments and creeds and disciplines? If there is an inner light to guide us, why rely on words of Scripture? If the divine spirit speaks to the soul, what need of ordained ministers to explain the truth? Such questions as these came to one and another traveller along the highway of religious history in moments of contemplation in study or monastery. Bernard of Clairvaux and Richard of Saint Victor, Thomas à Kempis and John Tauler, belong in that company between 1100 and 1500.

The Protestant Reformation regarded the Bible as a light of knowledge and a source of authority in religion. Puritans quibbled over forms and ceremonies. It was certain that the time would come when some one would pronounce these worthless and consign them to the rubbish heap, and so carry the revolt from the Catholic Church to the farthest point of radicalism. The man who outran Puritanism in England and reminded Christians again of the mystical quality of true religion was George Fox.

George Fox was the son of a weaver of Leicester-shire and of a mother whose family had come through the sufferings of persecution in the time of Queen Mary. The boy was born at Fenny Drayton in 1624. It was near the close of the reign of James I, between the date of settlement of Pilgrim Plymouth and of the Bay settlements about Boston. The Thirty Years' War was on in Germany. These events were to play their part in the history of Fox and his fellow Friends, but he had not dreamed of them when he grew from infancy into boyhood. Unlike most famous Englishmen of the seventeenth century, he did not feel strongly the moulding influence of the conformist Church of England. As a boy he sat under the preaching of a Puritan minister who became a thoroughgoing Presbyterian, and as a man he broke from all connection with organized religion to lead a movement along the mystic way of religious insight.

George was apprenticed to a master in leather manu-facture, but much of the time he was tending sheep. It is easy to imagine the sober youth herding sheep on the English hillside and meditating about the truth of religion, as David brooded while he watched his flock among the hills of Judea. He was characterized by serious purpose and truthfulness. He was not so out of touch with the social affairs of his day but that he could attend a country fair and enjoy its diversions, but one day when he was nineteen years old he went home from a fair where business had taken him with dissatisfaction gnawing at his heart. He had enjoyed a drink of beer with certain Puritan friends, but as he meditated on the way home he was troubled that religion did not take hold of their lives more completely than it seemed to.

During the three years that followed the youthful Fox went through a period of searching for truth, as Luther did before he came to the conclusion that the substance of religion was personal faith in Christ. But Luther spent the years in the monastery, and turned to the Bible for instruction. Fox left home and wandered over the country, trying to find peace of mind. Disappointed, he returned home lest his relatives should be troubled about him. He talked with the minister, but got no comfort. Then he went off again, trying the way of friendship and charity. In his spirit of friendliness he was like Francis of Assisi, but he was no Catholic saint. He walked in solitude with his Bible as companion. He talked with ministers of the Independent churches, but his thinking did not jibe with theirs. He began to get gleams of light in the thought that to be a Christian was to be neither Catholic nor Protestant, educated or uneducated, but to have the presence of Christ in the heart. At length the Spirit spoke peace to him such as he had not found with men.

From that time on he listened to the inner voice and followed the inner light. He had little education, but he could read the Bible, and that confirmed him in his belief. He enjoyed occasions of mystical exuberance when he was conscious that God kept him from temptation and offered him the delights of communion. He still travelled about, and soon convinced others of the reality of the spiritual life, and of the possibility of living in perfect harmony with God. Puritans with their belief in human sinfulness denounced such teaching, but Fox maintained his opinions against all comers.

Fox became an evangelist of his gospel to the people of England. He was not free from misgivings at times. He was narrow-minded and inclined to fanaticism. He was so strong in his denunciation of the Puritans who opposed him that he aroused bitter hostility. But even his enemies came to see that he was sincere in his convictions, and those who did not agree with him respected him for his courage and zeal. He was consistent in his opposition to formalism. He was so democratic that he would not make the distinctions of speech that were customary in conversation. It was only " thee " and " thou " between Friends. He was a lover of peace and taught his followers that it was wrong to engage in war. He refused to take an oath. He wore the plainest of clothes. These peculiarities of the preacher were adopted by his followers and became Quaker peculiarities. They were called Quakers by those who ridiculed because they often trembled emotionally when they spoke publicly.

In the troubled days of the Commonwealth and the intolerant monarchy that followed George Fox witnessed to the faith that was in him, travelling widely in England. He won converts to his ideas. Before 1650 a group of Friends near Derby established a " meeting," which served as a bond to unite them to one another. The word " meeting " had a double sense. It was the gathering of Friends for worship, and it was a substitute for " church," because they had no ecclesiastical organization or ordained ministers.

The evangelist was interested in the application of religion to social relations. Whenever he had a feeling that he ought to champion somebody's cause, he started off on the errand, no matter where it might lead him. He protested against stingy wages to servants. He went to innkeepers and urged them not to make their customers drunk. He went to the markets and denounced dishonesty in trade. He was unconventional in his religion. He would not worship with other people in the churches, but he would march into an assembly and interrupt the minister to utter his own contrary opinions. Naturally he suffered arrest, and again and again was shut up in prison, only to be released after a time and resume his wandering and preaching. Frequently he was abused by those who scoffed at him. Often he had to sleep in the open air. In Westmoreland he preached sitting on a rock to an audience of a thousand persons.

The Quaker movement would have had small results if it had not enlisted a few persons of better social position who could give it respectability. One of these was Robert Barclay, an educated man of Scotch family who was drawn to the Friends by their friendliness and who became the defender of the new sect in his Apology. Another was William Penn, son of an English admiral and himself the founder of the Pennsylvania colony in America. A third was Margaret Fell. She was the wife of Judge Fell of Swarthmore Hall in the north of England, who entertained travellers on religious errands, and to the Hall came Fox on one of his journeys. He soon persuaded the wife that his teaching of the inner light was true doctrine, and the Judge permitted Fox to hold meetings in his house. Swarthmore Hall became a place of refuge for the persecuted Quaker preachers.

Within five years of Fox's conversion sixty such preachers were evangelizing England. They suffered hardships of travel over the dangerous roads, but they were in greater danger from Church and State, both of which had little patience with such unconventional sectarians. Again and again Fox was put into prison, and others endured all kinds of indignities, but they kept preaching, and they found many persons who welcomed the personal experience of religion that they explained as an inner light of the soul. Harshly they wrote pamphlets against the forms of religion that they opposed, and as harshly came the replies, with such titles as *Hell Broken Loose: a History of the Quakers,* and *The Pilgrim's Progress from Quakerism to Christianity.*

The evangelists went everywhere over the country of England. Over the hills and the moors, from village to village of the interior or along the coast they travelled, stopping to challenge men in the fields or marching into a church service with their hats on, and interrupting the exercises to utter their own odd opinions. After a time they ventured to London where their converts became numerous enough to make it advisable to hire a large hall for the meetings besides many gatherings in private houses. Certain men

crossed over to Ireland and sowed the seed of their
doctrines there. A number of Friends made their way
to America. Several of them arrived in Boston where
they made themselves a nuisance. They were banished from the colony, but when several of them persisted in returning they were hung on Boston Common.

After Charles I became king in 1660 and the Church
of England was restored in its episcopal form, dissent
of every sort was banned. In a succession of intolerant laws Parliament expressed the will of the rulers, and many suffered because of their independency.
Among these was John Bunyan, whose experiences in
Bedford jail caused him to write *Pilgrim's Progress,*
and Richard Baxter, the Presbyterian author of *The
Saint's Everlasting Rest.* Quakers were treated
severely. During the twenty years of King Charles's
reign more than thirteen thousand of them were imprisoned, two hundred of them were transported as
slaves, and three hundred and forty died victims of
ill-treatment. Persecution brought out the fine qualities of the loyal Friends and commended their faith to
some who would not have been interested in it otherwise. It was during the period of severe persecution
that both Barclay and Penn became Quaker recruits.

In 1669 Fox married Margaret Fell, who had become
a widow. She had been a tower of strength to the
Quakers, keeping them in touch with one another by
means of a wide correspondence which passed through
her hands. She did not escape imprisonment, but she
had social influence and used it for the benefit of her
people. Her marriage to Fox added to his strength.

Both of them were so devoted to the movement that they did not allow the marriage to hamper their activities, and Fox was soon off on longer journeys. These carried him to the Continent and even to America. He found Friends in the free colony of Rhode Island, preached on Long Island and settled differences among the members of the meetings. He passed south to Maryland and Virginia, busy with the same errands. He even preached to the Indians. His American journeys were made in spite of the handicap of ill-kept inns, unbridged streams, and rough trails, but he put up with all inconveniences and discomforts because he was doing the Lord's work. From the South he went to the West Indies. His observations of slavery made him an enemy of the system.

George Fox was a forerunner of Wesley and Whitefield as an evangelist, for many years journeying over England, surviving hard experiences, persisting in his preaching and organizing, never idle, never in despair, until as he approached the end of his life he could feel that his work was done, and could look out over the land dotted with Quaker meetings and enjoying at last freedom from persecution as a result of the passage of the Toleration Act in 1689. The Quaker movement reached its climax about that time. It seemed to thrive on persecution. At first fanatical, it became sobered with the years, until others thought less of the fanaticism than of the noble spirit of the Friends and their contributions to social welfare.

George Fox died in London in 1691.

The Quaker movement started in a very simple way.

It is not to be supposed that Fox intended to start a new denomination. He found enlightenment and joy in his own heart, and he was convinced that only through such an experience could religion become real. Doubtless he hoped that the whole Church would become persuaded that the essence of religion was such an inner experience. He evangelized with that purpose. But his teachings were not welcomed. His conduct was too irregular. He and others like him were imprisoned and their families suffered. In order to provide help for them in a systematic way the first " meeting " came into existence. This was followed by others which became local organizations for worship and for discipline. These meetings were congregations of Friends, and were really local churches. They did not have appointed ministers like other Dissenters, but depended upon the instruction of those who were moved by the Spirit to speak or pray. Those who were most approved were sanctioned by the people and recognized as their religious leaders. As the new teaching spread general meetings were held to which attendants came from many places, collections were made for those who needed help, and discussions were held with Baptists, and with the Ranters who were especially troublesome to the Friends. Out of these early associations came the system of meetings that was later in vogue in England and America.

The Quakers found their way to America within a decade of the time when George Fox began to preach. They were pushed out of Massachusetts and Connecticut, and some of them went farther south. In the colony of Rhode Island they became strong enough to prevent Rhode Island from joining with other colonies in the Indian war.   Roger Williams challenged George Fox to debate with him, but Fox was off on his travels before it could take place.   Then Williams wrote *George Fox digged out of his Burrows*, and the Quaker issued a reply under the title *A New England Firebrand Quenched*.   But Quakers were prominent in the colony, and when the Baptists founded a college in Rhode Island a century later Quakers were given representation on the board of trustees.

On Long Island they found an abiding place, though the government of New Netherlands was hostile for a time.   The visit of Fox to the South doubled the membership of the Quaker meetings there.   In Maryland and Virginia the Episcopal parsons were contented with the forms of religious worship, but the people longed for better spiritual nourishment and responded to the preaching of Fox.

By 1681 William Penn founded the Quaker colony of Pennsylvania.   Protected by a royal charter, the Quakers were able to organize a colony of their own with such generous provisions for other persecuted sects that Pennsylvania became a polyglot colony with many representatives of many Protestant dissenting groups from the Continent.   The City of Brotherly Love on the Schuylkill River became a prosperous town, destined to be the first capital of the American nation.   The Quakers were industrious and thrifty and the colony was an unquestioned success.   In the centre of the coast settlements it became a nursery of peace and good citizenship, less fiery in defense of political rights than Massachusetts or Virginia, but a leader in philanthropy and all humane matters.

The Friends have been pioneers of an applied religion. They believed slavery to be wrong, and used peaceful means to check and relieve it. They were among the first to propose prison reform and to try to check intemperance. Believing that war is wrong, they have maintained consistently a determination not to bear arms, but they have been conspicuous in the relief of those who have suffered from war or other distress. Judging by their fruits the critic may not judge harshly George Fox and his Friends.

9

JONATHAN EDWARDS

NEW ENGLAND was a Puritan country. Its first settlers were inspired to hardy endeavour by the energy and iron determination of John Calvin and his successors. They rejected his presbyterian system of church organization for congregational independency, but they kept his belief in the sovereign will of God and the necessity of character in man. In Massachusetts and Connecticut they united Church and State, and made religion a powerful factor in colonial affairs. But as decades passed and the original settlers died, the zeal for religion grew less. The members of the churches were not always persons of religious experience or of strong conviction, and many families were moving out of reach of the churches as the colonies expanded north and west.

Massachusetts founded Harvard College and Connecticut organized Yale College to educate men for the colonial ministry, but the building of meeting-houses could not keep pace with the advancing frontier. Indian difficulties and wars, and the absorption of the people in subduing the wilderness drew public attention from the Church. This state of affairs caused grave concern to ministers like Cotton Mather at Boston. They lamented the decline of religious interest, and they wrote voluminously on religious subjects, but they saw no way to make the people less worldly. A

Connecticut minister wrote: " In great measure we in this wilderness have lost our first love. . . . We do not walk with God as our fathers did, and hence we are continually from year to year under His rebukes." About the same time Increase Mather of Boston said: " If the begun apostasy should proceed as fast the next thirty years as it has done this last, surely it will come to that in New England that the most conscientious people therein will think themselves concerned to gather churches out of churches."

It became clear after a time that the only way to arrest the attention of the people was by more pungent preaching. Ministers began to get a response to their appeals. Revivals of spiritual interest occurred in different localities. New members were welcomed into the churches. Among the evangelistic preachers of the eighteenth century was the young minister of the Congregational church at Northampton, Jonathan Edwards. Northampton was in the valley of the Connecticut River, where some of the earliest settlers established the Massachusetts frontier. In the eighteenth century its Congregational church was one of the leading Puritan organizations. Edwards was a young man when he accepted the pastorate, but he grew up with his parish and made his ministry notable through all the colonies. He was to become famous first for his preaching power, and then for his philosophical ability and his interpretation of the Calvinistic theology.

Jonathan Edwards was the son of the minister of the church in South Windsor, Connecticut, farther down the Connecticut valley. His mother was the daughter of Solomon Stoddard, the well-known minister at Northampton. Their boy was born in 1703, the year of the birth of John Wesley, the founder of Methodism. The only boy in a family of ten sisters he could not grow up selfish or a recluse. His father started his education in the study of the manse, but it is easy to believe that his mother and sisters had a part in shaping his character. His life was fashioned far differently from that of George Fox. He showed precocious intellectual ability, and he was fond of nature. It was not to be his destiny to wander about the countryside as an evangelist of the inner light, but he had in his soul a witness to the reality of religion, and he resolved to be a preacher, like his father.

The proper course for such a purpose was a college education, and at the age of thirteen Jonathan went to Yale, graduating subsequently at the head of his class. He delighted to read and ponder upon the profound problems of human life and destiny, and he was glad to continue his studies two more years at Yale. About the time of his graduation the young man had a distinct consciousness of the meaning of God to him, and from that time he had an affection for God and a lively sense of His glory and majesty which furnished him hours of contemplation and mystical satisfaction. He resolved to devote his life to the glory of God.

He passed a brief apprenticeship in preaching in New York City but he returned soon to New Haven as a tutor in the college, and while there courted Sarah Pierpont, daughter of the minister, who presently became his wife. She was a young woman of deep religious feeling and strength of character. She was a true helpmeet to her ministerial husband, and reared a large family of children. Shortly before his marriage Edwards went to Northampton to be assistant to his grandfather Stoddard, and two years later he became sole pastor.

Northampton had not forgotten the sermons of their aged minister, or his invitation to share in the Lord's Supper as a means of grace, even if they were not conscious that they were really Christians. But the sermons of the grandson searched their inmost hearts, put them on the rack of conscience, shook them in imagination over the fires of hell, convinced them that they were sinners, and warned them to repent and pray for salvation. Edwards did not win attention by his magnetic personality, powerful voice, or animated way of preaching. In all these he was defective. It was his solemn manner, vivid description, and convincing arguments that drove his message home to the hearts of his people.

Such preaching to people who believed unquestioningly in the doctrines of Calvinism had a fearsome effect. Some were almost beside themselves with fear of eternal punishment. Others were thrown into despondency lest they had not been elected by God to be saved. So remarkable were the evidences of an emotional upheaval that Edwards wrote an account of it to interested persons in England, calling his treatise *Narrative of Surprising Conversions*. The whole community was stirred, and most of the people professed

conversion and joined the church. The whole community was sobered by the experience, and revivals
spread to other towns. But the usual reaction
occurred in another decline of religious interest.

Edwards continued his forceful sermons, and after
six years another New England revival broke out, inspired principally by the preaching of George Whitefield, a visitor from England. Whitefield was an
orator of great power over the human emotions. He
spoke in the churches and to immense audiences out-
of-doors. Crowds of people left their farms and
poured into the village where he was to preach. They
listened to him spellbound, and yielded to his en-
treaties to put themselves right with God. In 1740
Whitefield made a preaching tour from the South to
New England, and he stimulated new interest in religion.

After Whitefield became known in America as a
popular preacher news of his approach was enough to
gather a large assembly. In Connecticut a story is
told of a farmer who left his plough in the furrow and
mounted a horse to ride twelve miles to the place where
Whitefield was advertised to speak. He drove his
horse to the limit to reach the scene quickly, and as
he drew near he overtook people driving in from all
directions until the whole countryside seemed to be in
motion. Eager expectancy greeted the speaker and
intense feeling accompanied and followed his sermon.
Large numbers of people were compelled to think
seriously of life, and thousands joined the churches.
Certain of the Puritan ministers of a conservative dis-

position did not like the new methods of evangelism and wrote and spoke against it, but it worked, and that was enough to commend it to a great many. The sympathizers with the revivalists were nicknamed New Lights.

The feeling between the more conservative churches and the New Lights was so strong in some localities as to result in the organization of Separatist churches in Massachusetts and Connecticut. The people of those churches were stirred emotionally, but they were not particular about an educated ministry. They were sometimes burdened with taxes for the support of the Congregational system which they had abandoned, and to escape taxation a few such Separatist churches became Baptist. The Baptist churches most of the time were exempted from taxation. In the long run most of the Separatist churches died or drifted back into the Congregational fold.

The vivid experiences of this new outbreak of emotion led Edwards to write one of his most thoughtful books on the nature of true religion. He was not favourable to emotional extravagances, and argued that only those affections are worthy that are the result of the action of the Holy Spirit upon the heart, and that result in a life of rectitude and earnest Christian purpose. For twenty years the Northampton pastor kept his commanding influence over his people, then troubles thickened. He did not agree with his grandfather Stoddard that it was proper to open the communion service freely to all comers, and when he refused admittance to certain persons and unwisely

attempted to discipline others in the spirit of Calvin,
the church at Northampton turned against Edwards,
and he moved to a new location in 1750.

Driven thus from his home and church when he was
nearly fifty years old, with a family of ten children
needing his protection and care, Edwards did not find
it easy to decide as to his future course of action. But
he was not without friends. Dr. John Erskine was a
leader among the Calvinists of Scotland. He sent
books to Edwards, urged him to use his time to write,
and later took upon himself the task of seeing through
the press the theological volumes that Edwards produced. Gifts of money came from other Scotch
friends. Mrs. Edwards and her daughters did all that
they possibly could to replenish the family purse.
There was even a proposal to Edwards to emigrate to
Scotland, where he should have a Presbyterian church.
But the occasion passed, and within a few months he
became pastor of a small rural church at Stockbridge
among the Berkshire Hills. He was also made a missionary to the Housatonic Indians, by appointment of
the Board of Indian Affairs at Boston, assisted in his
support by the Anglicans. About the same time he
was invited to a church in Virginia, and certain individuals would have organized an independent church
in Northampton, if he had consented to return.
Meantime, one of the daughters of the family married
Reverend Aaron Burr, the youthful president of
Princeton College, and became mother of the brilliant
but erratic Aaron Burr, later Vice-President of the
United States.

At Stockbridge Edwards had leisure to study, and he was at the height of his intellectual maturity. For seven years he worked and wrote, producing the greatest books that America had yet contributed to theology, until in 1758 he accepted the presidency of Princeton College, but within a few weeks he was dead at the age of fifty-five.

It would be natural to expect that theological writing would be at its best at Cambridge or New Haven instead of on the edge of the forest. Luther and Calvin wrote in a university environment. The Puritan leaders were trained at the English universities, chiefly at Cambridge. But the mind of Edwards was self-stimulating. He was a thinker while still in his teens. He had written on theology while pastor at Northampton. The quiet life at Stockbridge with its minimum of pastoral duties gave him time to think, and his tastes led him to meditation on the great problems which the mind of man has wrestled with. As a result of his meditation and the publication of his books he became recognized as the greatest intellect in America, and as the leader in a school of thought that accepted certain modifications of Calvinism but maintained it zealously as a system of truth.

Jonathan Edwards was an exponent of a modified Calvinism which became known as the New England theology. The Calvinistic doctrine was accepted by the Puritans as a correct theology. Central in it was the idea that man was helpless, but in the hands of a sovereign God. This meant that a man had no power to choose the good, to move in the direction of God and heaven, but he must wait for God to move him. Yet to preach the terrors of the Judgment and the horrors of hell to human beings bound and helpless was calculated to make them hopeless if not insane. Edwards as an evangelistic preacher saw that Calvinism must be modified to the extent of finding a place for human action. As he thought about it, it seemed to him that a man had a natural power to get right with God, if he felt so inclined, and it was the minister's business to make him inclined. Yet for all that, man has no moral power, for even the inclination is dependent on God's revelation of Himself as worth serving. In this way Edwards saved Calvinism and found room for evangelism. His book on *Freedom of the Will* was an exposition of his ideas on that subject.

Edwards stressed another principle that became prominent in the New England theology. This was the principle of good will, which he called benevolence. It is the good will of God which makes Him try to save men, and it is the good will of man to God and all His creatures that is the heart of the spiritual life. In this he was getting at the heart of the teaching of Jesus, though his thought about the process was too mechanical.

The influence of Edwards upon ministers in his own Congregational denomination was powerful. He erred in overstressing certain elements of a theology that was based on a misinterpretation of human nature and the nature of God. But in the men whom he indoctrinated he founded a school of thought which continued for a century and more, in the New England churches and religious schools. He was opposed by a liberal group of ministers who believed that a moral process was going on in man, and if his conduct was exemplary no act of regeneration was necessary. Such difference of opinion is always apparent between those who emphasize God's part in man's salvation from sin and low levels of life and those who emphasize what man can do for himself. Neither sufficiently realized the part of both working together, or sensed God as working within men to accomplish His will. The differences of opinion widened until Unitarianism made a division among the Congregationalists.

Subsequent champions of the New England theology perpetuated the theological achievements of Edwards. About the time that Edwards was enjoying the revival at Northampton Joseph Bellamy graduated at Yale. Soon after that event he became pastor of a village church at Bethlem in Connecticut, where he was content to stay for fifty-two years until his death in 1790. He was an effective preacher and might have had better positions if he had wished. But he made his mark as a writer and teacher of theology. He had studied for a time with Edwards. In those days prospective ministers often lived as pupils in the home of a minister of reputation. Bellamy himself soon was receiving such students of theology and during his long pastorate no less than sixty received his instruction. His most influential book was *True Religion Delineated*, in which he presented his opinions about the atonement which differed slightly from his master Edwards. In other respects he was his understudy.

Like Bellamy, Samuel Hopkins was a Connecticut boy and a Yale graduate six years later than Bellamy. He too was a disciple of Edwards and perhaps his most intimate friend. He is considered a second founder of the New England theology. For twenty-two years he was a rural minister at Great Barrington, Massachusetts, where he was a neighbour of Edwards, and for thirty-three years he occupied the influential pulpit of the Congregational church in Newport, Rhode Island. At Newport he denounced the slave trade, although Newport men made money out of it. He contended for temperance and for other community reforms. But it was as a thinker that he deserved his reputation as the interpreter of the New Divinity, which was the old Calvinism with an emphasis on repentance and faith rather than on moral conduct as a means of salvation.

The theological ideas of Jonathan Edwards, Joseph Bellamy, and Samuel Hopkins were developed under the spur of practical need. They saw people in the New England communities interested in other things than religion, and when summoned to religious concern excusing themselves on the ground that they could do nothing for themselves because God was sovereign. Edwards found a way out by declaring that man had a natural ability to choose the best course. Bellamy pried loose the rigid Calvinism by declaring that the atonement of Christ was general in its scope rather than limited, though only applied to those whom God had elected to save. These seemed to be only slight gains, leaving the sinner still in the hands of God, but they made it easier to preach repentance.

Other interpreters of New England theology followed these first three, among whom was a son of Edwards, known in history as Jonathan Edwards the Younger. He had a career similar to that of his father. As time passed slight divergences appeared, but the main doctrines were maintained sturdily against the liberal tendencies of the late eighteenth and early nineteenth centuries. The New England theology was in the main a development of Congregationalism in Connecticut and western Massachusetts, but it was dominant in the eastern theology of Andover Seminary also.

The career of Edwards is an example of men who even on the frontier of civilization make their mark because they have an original contribution to make to life or thought. Jonathan Edwards ranks as the greatest thinker among New England Puritans in the colonial period.

10

JOHN WESLEY

WHILE Jonathan Edwards was stirring Northampton with his fiery sermons a young Englishman at Oxford was preparing to go as a missionary to the new American colony of Georgia. He had been active as a religious leader while a graduate fellow of the University, and he believed that he might be useful among the orphans and ne'er-do-weels of the philanthropic experiment overseas. No one would have imagined then that in John Wesley, the Georgia missionary, England was to find the most popular prophet of the age, but the prophet was in the making.

John Wesley was born in 1703, the birth year of Jonathan Edwards, in the rural village of Epworth. In that place his father, Samuel Wesley, was rector of the parish church. His mother, Susannah, was a sensible, conscientious woman, and a mother of nineteen children. Both husband and wife were of Puritan stock, but they were regular members of the Church of England. The time of John's birth was a period of regularity in religion. The commotions of the seventeenth century were long since passed. The Toleration Act of 1689 had given peace to the distracted country, and when Dissent was no longer persecuted it ceased to grow. It was not good form to get excited over

religion. Spiritual fervour was not a characteristic of
the churches. Certain men like William Law, author
of *A Serious Call to a Holy Life,* were spiritually
minded. There was an intellectual strength among
men of the clergy like Bishop Butler that was not found
a century earlier. But religion did not grip the lives
of the people, whether it was the religion of the Established Church or of the Dissenting chapel.

The Church of England never had filled the old
Catholic forms with the vitalizing breath of a personal
religious experience. Many were the individuals who
gathered comfort and strength from the Church, but
religion was a corporate affair which one accepted without question along with other gifts of civilization.
Calvinistic Puritanism stressed the personal side of
religion, but it was marked by order and severity
rather than by feeling and fervour, and it was a religion
of the middle class. The mass of Englishmen were not
affected by it, and they were only indifferently influenced by the Established Church. The working people whether in town or country were neglected and
their children allowed to grow up in ignorance, while
the adults indulged in the gross pleasures of the tavern
and the cockpit. Drunkenness was the most common
form of vice. To evangelize these folk was the task of
the Methodists.

John Wesley was the child of good fortune. At the
age of ten he escaped burning to death at home, which
always seemed to him a special act of God's mercy.
In spite of pecuniary difficulties in so large a family he
was able to attend the well-known Charter-house School

in London, and go on to the University of Oxford. The religious influences of his home had made him seriously minded, and he was ordained to the Anglican ministry at the age of twenty-two. But his religion was formal. He tried to do his duty as a Christian by visiting persons in distress, by religious reading, and by the leadership of a Holy Club of congenial spirits at Oxford, where he remained for a time.

In 1735 he was persuaded to go with his brother Charles to America, and there he worked some of the formal religion out of his system, but he did not succeed as a missionary, and his expectation of doing good to the Indians came to nothing. He failed in tact and courtesy in some of his personal relations, and presently he found it advisable to return home. On the voyage he had conversations about religion with certain Moravians on board, and he felt a lack of spirituality in himself, when he realized how poised and peaceful were their minds and how sincere was their confidence in God.

Soon after his return Wesley dropped into a religious meeting in London on a certain May evening. It was a gathering of one of the religious societies which just then evidenced the soul aspirations of not a few Anglicans. The same spirit was to be felt there that was apparent in the life of the Moravians. As time wore on Wesley became deeply affected, until at a quarter before nine, as he said, he felt his heart strangely warmed and his life changed by a consciousness of his soul's salvation. From that time Wesley looked for an opportunity to bring that same experience to others.

He was puzzled to know how to tell his story. He was the rector of no church. He could not have contented himself with settling down in a single parish. His heart was on fire for God, but the Church of England had no method of evangelism by which he could visit numerous churches. He secured one or two opportunities to preach, but he showed too much enthusiasm to suit the steady-going ecclesiastical authorities, and he found himself without an audience and the doors of the churches shut against him. Then he adopted an innovation in method, though reluctantly. George Whitefield, who had been a member of the Holy Club at Oxford and was winning a reputation as a preacher, had tried the experiment of preaching out-of-doors with great success. He urged Wesley to try the same method and at last Wesley decided to follow so good an example.

It is strange that the method of Jesus in studying amid the scenery of nature and revealing nature's God to men should have been used so little in Christian preaching. Crowds of working folk gathered about Wesley, though he preached in a brickyard. He preached his first sermon to them on the text that Jesus chose at Nazareth: " The Spirit of the Lord is upon me because he hath anointed me to preach the gospel to the poor; he hath sent me to heal the broken-hearted, to preach deliverance to the captives, the recovery of sight to the blind; to set at liberty them that are bruised; to preach the acceptable year of the Lord." At Kingswood four miles out of Bristol he talked to the British miners until the tears made white furrows in their sooty cheeks. His preaching marked the beginning of Methodism.

The Methodist movement was an evangelical mission to the common people of England. Wesley spoke out of the fulness of his own heart experience, and preached a crucified and risen Christ to men and women who knew that they were sinners and needed forgiveness. Sticklers for good order and precedent, such as Wesley had been once, criticised his conduct, but he was happy in his success and believed that God's favour was with him. He went to London and back again in that year 1739, while his brother Charles, who had had a striking experience of conversion, stayed in the capital, and Whitefield, who was heart and soul with Wesley in everything but Wesley's Arminian doctrine, plunged zealously into revival efforts in Wales and later in America.

As a preacher John Wesley was straightforward, outspoken, and earnest. He played upon the emotions and then called for an act of will, committing men to a Christian life. There was no beating about the bush. The doctrine that he preached was not Calvinistic. Wesley did not believe in man's helplessness, or in God's hard-heartedness. God was in Christ reconciling the world unto Himself. Let men come and be reconciled. He pointed out plainly the consequences of neglect. A man would better not take chances. Hell was vividly real and dangerously near. But God was loving and had provided a Saviour. And to such preaching Wesley got response, as Edwards had. Men and women screamed and fainted in distress of soul, but most of them found their way through to peace and joy. It was heroic treatment of souls, as surgery is of bodies, but it was necessary in immoral England in the eighteenth century, and it achieved results. Learned discussions on deistic belief and rational evidences of religion were well enough for university classes or London drawing-rooms. They could not win the masses of the people. But the old story of Jesus and His love was the never-failing magnet of Methodism.

Whether the Methodist movement saved England from another French Revolution it is impossible to say. But it converted many thousands of Englishmen to new purposes and stimulated new interests. They began to live better. They grumbled less about their lot. And they did not turn bolshevist when the Revolution came on the Continent.

Wesley soon found it necessary to follow up his evangelistic methods with some sort of organization by which he could cultivate the seeds of religion that had been sown. He organized religious societies. He had no intention to divorce his movement from the Church, but the Church was not supplying the needful spiritual nourishment for his converts. He hit upon the unconventional method of grouping his converts in small classes. The members agreed to meet together every week for the confession of their faults and for prayer. It became necessary to have a place for meetings in Bristol, which was the centre of his movement, and to pay for the new building every Methodist class underwrote the scheme with a pledge of a penny a week per member. Methodism rarely has had great wealth at its disposal, but the combined contributions of small givers has reached an enormous aggregate.

In order to create a feeling of good fellowship between societies and to provide preaching, circuits were arranged for visitation and superintendents were appointed, similar to Anglican bishops. Though no official body gave him authority Wesley was dictator of the movement, as Calvin was at Geneva, and as was William Booth of the Salvation Army, which came out of Methodism in the nineteenth century. Wesley was handicapped by lack of leaders. Not many of the Anglican clergy were sympathetic with him, and he was forced to fall back upon laymen, so that Methodism was a lay movement in the main during the period of its development. Wesley bore the heaviest of the burdens. He formulated a Discipline. He carried the oversight of all the churches. He travelled about preaching his message. He started schools for the children of illiterate coal miners, believing with the American revivalist Moody that education and religion were both necessary.

All English roads led to London, as ancient roads led to Rome. The Methodist movement would not begin to reach its goal until it went to London. At Moorfields near by Wesley found an opportunity to preach, and he purchased an old cannon foundry to use for an assembly hall. He decided to make it Methodist headquarters, borrowed money to make repairs, and presently found himself in possession of a large building one hundred and twenty by a hundred feet, containing a chapel to accommodate an audience of fifteen hundred, a schoolroom, a smaller room for group meetings, and a book room for the sale of Wesley's publications. Upstairs Wesley had living quarters for himself and his widowed mother as long as she lived, and rooms for assistant preachers and a household staff. From the year 1740 the Foundry in London was the centre of Methodist organization. Then Wesley went to the north of England on a preaching mission and established Yorkshire headquarters at Newcastle.

The establishment of Methodist centres of organization looked very much like building up a separate denominational organization, but Wesley was opposed to separation from the Church of England. He hoped that Methodism might kindle a new life within the old church. He was unwilling to provide for the ordinances of baptism or the Lord's Supper outside of the parish churches, nor would he ordain ministers or bishops. He called his groups the United Societies.

The Methodist movement was popular among the lowly, like primitive Christianity, and similar circumstance made occasional charity necessary. Records of one of the Methodist societies of London kept for more than thirty years show that a sum of fifteen thousand dollars was applied to charity in a little more than twenty years. Wesley in early life had given some time to the study of medicine, and he took a personal interest in the sick, visiting them, dosing them, applying electrical experiments, and giving hygienic and dietetic advice. He laid down four rules for voluntary visitors. They were: Be plain and open in dealing with souls. Be mild, patient, tender. Be cleanly in all you do for them. Be not nice. He established a dispensary at the London Foundry. He thus applied religion to every-day need.

As early as the days of the Holy Club at Oxford Wesley had been interested in the inmates of the prisons, many of whom were there for nothing worse than debt. More than once he stood with men on the scaffold or talked intimately with them in their prison cells. Many times he preached in the jails, and pointed out the worth of an individual man. His interest in the poor led him to try experiments in providing employment, an enterprise that has been imitated by Morgan Memorial Church in Boston and similar institutional churches elsewhere. Wesley selected a few needy women to card and spin cotton under the direction of a teacher, continuing the experiment for four months to the end of winter, and the plan nearly paid for itself. He also established a loan fund for which he solicited his friends, and in this way cheated the pawnshop out of some of its victims. Repayment was made in weekly instalments, and it worked so well that the plan was expanded and made a permanent feature of Methodism.

As often as possible Wesley was off on an evangelistic tour. For decades he rode horseback into all parts of England, thinking as he rode, preaching wherever he could gather an audience, visiting and heartening the societies, indefatigable in his attention to his task day in and day out. He endured inconveniences, even hardships, but his spiritual energy did not fail, and his body served him to a ripe old age.

It became continually clearer to most of the leaders that Methodism was destined to separate from the Church of England. One step after another Wesley was compelled to take, though unwillingly, that led away from the old organization. He appointed lay preachers without any authority from his Anglican bishop. He called conferences of ministers without any authority but his own. He at length administered the sacrament in his chapels when they had not been duly consecrated as churches. He appointed superintendents of Methodism in America. At last in 1784 he even ordained men to the ministry. He justified himself by the necessity, saying: " If any one will point out a more rational and scriptural way of feeding and guiding these poor sheep in the wilderness, I will gladly embrace it. At present I cannot see any better method than I have taken."

John Wesley outlived most of his associates in Methodism. Long after he was eighty years old he was still itinerating. When he went to his last conference held at Bristol the Methodist societies numbered two hundred and forty with 135,000 members. Five hundred and forty preachers were on the circuits. On the second day of March, 1791, the end came to his life in London, and he was buried in his own chapel burying ground across the street from the resting place of John Bunyan and Isaac Watts and his own mother in Bunhill fields.

Charles Wesley, a younger brother, was a powerful

aid to the progress of Methodism. A member with his brother John of the Holy Club at Oxford, he accompanied him to Georgia and back, and became a popular preacher among the Methodists, though overshadowed by his brother. But he is best known as a hymn writer. He put into words the vivid experiences of souls on fire with the Spirit of God. He ran the whole gamut of religious emotion, and expressed for the multitude of Methodists convictions and feelings that were eager for utterance. Many of his hymns carried more power of conviction than sermons. The people committed the words to memory, enlarged the vocabulary of their speech with the words and phrases of the hymns, and were strengthened by their doctrine and cheered by their message of hope. In 1749 two volumes of sacred song were published in Charles Wesley's name, and from that time to this his hymns have filled a prominent place in the hymnology of the Christian Church. Wesley and Watts still contribute the largest number of hymns to the hymnals of the evangelical churches.

The story of Methodism is one of magnificent achievement. Its message has gone to all the world, and its organization has gained strength in every continent. It is the most numerous of all Protestant bodies in America. Everywhere it has had a moral and social effect upon the life of the people. It has inspired other denominations. Even the Church of England was touched with the spirit of Methodism, and the Evangelical party became a champion of philanthropy and social reform. It was the fervour of

Methodism that stirred the sense of obligation to evangelize pagan peoples. On the western frontier of America the circuit rider carried on the home mission enterprise. Methodists have been leaders in the social application of religion. Popular education has been encouraged ever since Wesley started his schools for the poor children. Methodist academies and colleges are sown thickly across the broad acres of America.

Finally John Wesley made religion primarily a matter of personal experience of the individual with God. Luther had learned that a man cannot depend upon a priest or a church to practise religion for him. Calvin had maintained a theology that made every man equal before God and alike the object of His frown. Wesley caught the message of Jesus that the Saviour died for every man, that grace was free, that God loves the sinner, that Christ saves through the power of His life and death, and that through the Spirit's power it is possible to win through to a glorious victory over the forces of life that thwart noble purpose, if they can. Methodism was the climax and triumph of the Reformation.

11

FRANCIS ASBURY

IN the little village of Wednesbury in Staffordshire Wesley met with some of the most bitter persecution that he had to endure. In those times there were many rough, lawless fellows who were glad of an excuse to stir up a brawl, and Methodist preaching supplied an opportunity. But out of Wednesbury came two young men who were to become illustrious leaders of Methodism. One of them was Francis Asbury.

Born in 1745 at Handsworth, the son of a gardener, he began to preach at Wednesbury when he was only seventeen years old. At that time Methodism was growing, and Wesley had need of all the recruits that he could obtain. He therefore made this local preacher one of the regular itinerants, and in 1771 sent him to America.

When Asbury was a boy of fifteen a company of German emigrants landed in New York. Disturbed by European wars, they had left their homes in the Rhineland and had gone to Ireland and settled in the county of Limerick. They were never happy there and they decided to go to America. In Ireland certain of them had been converted to Methodism, when that movement was making its way through the Emerald Isle. One of these was Philip Embury, a carpenter, who had exhorted his neighbours in the capac-

ity of a local preacher, and another was his cousin,
Barbara Heck. Arrived in New York they lost the
fervour of their Methodism at first, but after a little
Barbara Heck stirred up her cousin Embury to preach
in his house. Soon after this a certain Captain Webb
of the British army arrived and presently was preaching, with his sword laid across the pulpit. The crowds
that gathered to hear the novel preaching required
larger quarters, and the Methodists began to meet in
a sail loft. Webb contributed money generously for
the building of a church and raised more outside.
Then word was sent to England asking for volunteer
leaders.

Meantime another Irish Methodist, Robert Straw-
bridge, had settled in Maryland, built a log chapel
and aroused that region, and then carried Methodism
into the neighbouring colonies. Two men in England
answered the call for help, and Methodism began to
grow rapidly. From these small beginnings dates the
history of Methodism in America.

In 1771, two years after the first helpers had gone
to America, Wesley appointed Francis Asbury to go
out, and when Asbury was only twenty-five years old
Wesley made him superintendent of the infant
churches, and he located in Philadelphia, where the
Methodists had another church in a sail loft. But it
was not long before he was superseded by the arrival
of older men, and though he felt this as a grievance
he stuck to his task as a preacher, and in due time was
promoted.

It was characteristic of Asbury that he was self-confident and resented any slight or opposition. Rankin, his successor, had sent him as far away as he could, to Norfolk in Virginia, and three years after he had landed in America he was ordered back to England. But his destiny was otherwise. The Continental Congress was meeting already in Philadelphia, and by the time of the battle of Lexington all the Methodist preachers went back to England except Asbury. He cast in his fortunes with the colonists. John Wesley had no sympathy with the rebellious colonies, and Methodists were generally under suspicion. Not a few sought out new homes on the western frontier of colonization, and when the Revolution was over Asbury followed them with the ministrations of religion. With the new opportunity for growth the Methodists became impatient for full church organization, but Wesley was slow to see the necessity. Asbury counselled patience. At last Wesley yielded and in 1784 ordained Thomas Coke, a doctor of divinity, to take charge of Methodism in America, with power to ordain men to the American ministry. Wesley's reluctance had kept him from yielding to importunities for independent Methodist organization in England, but he could not resist the Americans any longer. Asbury welcomed Coke to America, and Coke after a long evangelistic tour summoned all the preachers to a conference at Baltimore.

The conference at Baltimore is known in Methodist history as the Christmas Conference of 1784. It met on the day before the holiday. Coke presented a letter from Wesley approving the organization of a Meth-

odist Episcopal church. Wesley had made it plain
that it was his wish that Coke and Asbury should be
the first bishops of the church in America. Coke had
been set apart to the ministry by Wesley himself, but
Asbury was only a lay preacher. It was necessary that
he be properly ordained. But Asbury would not accept an appointment as bishop unless he should be
elected to that office by the ministers. He knew the
democratic temper of the American people. He was
unanimously elected and then ordained on three successive days, first as deacon, second as elder, and then
as a bishop.

When the Methodist church was thus organized, the
future of America was uncertain. The war for independence had been won, but the former colonies were
disunited, there was no central government and
only a few millions of people. Their settlement
extended from Maine to Georgia, but they had only
recently passed over the mountains into Kentucky and
Tennessee. There was no conception of what an
American nation might be. Three years after the
Methodists organized at Baltimore the constitutional
convention of delegates from the new states met at
Philadelphia and adopted an instrument of government. Two years later still, in 1789, the machinery of
federal government began to move with George Washington as president of the United States.

By that time Methodist itinerant preachers were on
the move to reach the frontier settlements. They were
poor men, with little but a horse that they could call
their own, but they were rich in character and devo-

tion to their missionary purpose. They endured hardships in their long journeys over rough trails through the woods, but they treated the hardships as incidental to the work that they had volunteered to do for God. They were not bound by ecclesiastical conventions, for Methodism was breaking new ground. They found no meeting-houses in which to preach, no churches with regularly ordained ministries, few settlements that could boast of more than a few houses. They were frontier pioneers. But they preached the gospel of an itinerant evangelist of Palestine who had lived in the long ago, and they were content to live as He lived, homeless but not friendless, finding their reward in the day's work and in the consciousness of duty well done.

With the growth of settlement religious camp-meetings became popular. In the older parts of the country an awakening came to the Congregationalist and Presbyterian churches in a less emotional fashion, now that the frontier days of Edwards and Whitefield were over, but in the newer parts of the South and West the emotions had full play. The methods of evangelism of the illiterate frontier preachers were intended to appeal to the emotions, and those men did not feel satisfied unless they succeeded in awakening a response. The camp-meeting is an interesting study in religious psychology, but in spite of its extravagances it had profound moral and religious effects. The Cane Ridge camp-meeting in Kentucky is the best example of the camp-meeting of the period.

When a camp-meeting was arranged, the preparations were made by erecting a platform in the woods and spreading a tent roof over it. News of the meeting was carried from clearing to clearing. It was a welcome social event to isolated folk, and the people left every task to throng the meeting. All sorts of means of transportation were used. Various contrivances were adopted to provide for the week's needs. They pitched camp under the trees in tents or in the open. Excitement stirred their emotional natures from the opening meeting until the end. It passed like an electric current from mourning sinners kneeling at the altar to scoffers gambling on the outskirts. The emotional disturbance appeared in groans and tears and shouts of joy. Persons danced or rolled on the ground, jerked arms and legs, and even went insane. The shouting exhorters reminded them of the last summons to judgment, the flaming torches and camp fires of the terrors of hell. Swept away by the dramatic intensity of the scene, few could resist the words of warning and appeal. Thousands of persons were converted in the camp-meetings, but Asbury and other Methodist preachers put the converts on probation before admitting them to full membership in the churches.

It is easy to criticise the extravagant emotionalism of the camp-meetings, but their dramatic presentation of religion gripped the lives of the participants. They lived stripped to the elementals. They were accustomed to the rough ways and morals of the frontier. If religion was to make an effective appeal to them, it must be emotional, dramatic. But the camp-meeting was more than a gathering for religion. It supplied an opportunity for social intercourse for people who were starving for it. Many of them came from their lone clearings in the woods. They saw no white people for weeks at a time. They were hungry for companionship. At Cane Ridge and elsewhere they could banish their loneliness for a time and get the news from everywhere.

Bishop Asbury found his way to one of the earliest camp-meetings in Kentucky. He was on the move continually over the immense area of his superintendence. Regularly year after year, decade after decade, Asbury rode south through Philadelphia and Baltimore to the Carolinas, from there over the mountains into Tennessee and Kentucky, then back through the mountains to the upland counties of Virginia. Then he pushed north as far as Boston, and turning west struck out over the Berkshire Hills of western Massachusetts to the Hudson Valley which took him south again. During those journeys, doubly arduous because of the poor roads, many of them rough mountain trails, the missionary bishop endured innumerable hardships. Frequently he was soaked through with rain-storms, compelled to swim swollen streams, thrown from his horse and injured, forced to travel when seriously ill, finding no resting place except a crowded shack, yet with iron will he never faltered, and when the strength of old age was almost exhausted he still kept riding until death overtook him.

It is almost incredible that in fewer years Asbury should have covered more miles than did Wesley, and over a far rougher country. Nor did Asbury have the physical constitution of Wesley. Illness might have furnished him frequently with an excuse for abandoning the trail. Storms might well have daunted him, or the dangers of the road, but none of these moved him. His body might suffer, but his spirit ranged with God. Never well educated, he rode with books in his saddle-bags. When he could he read as he rode and in time he became a well-informed man, though never a great preacher. When he could not read, he gave himself to thought and to planning his next discourse. Of such stuff were the frontier evangelists made.

Asbury was not only a great missionary, but an ecclesiastical statesman as well. It was he who formed the general conference system in America by basing it on a permanent constitution. This was in 1808. Up to that time all ministers were expected to attend the general conference, but the increasing distances and number of preachers made attendance difficult, and there was a growing feeling that the conference should be made a delegated body. Opinion was divided almost evenly, and at one time there was danger that the conference might cease to cement together the Methodists of the country, but the persistence of Asbury and those who stood with him brought victory out of threatened defeat.

Asbury was an arbitrary dictator in his administration of denominational affairs, and he was unwilling to accept suggestions from others. This trait made him unpopular with some, and undoubtedly would have injured his influence seriously had he not been so conspicuous an example of absolute devotion to the work that he had been set apart to do. As it was James O'Kelley led a secession of Republican Methodists who resented Asbury's autocracy and wanted a Methodism that was more democratic, like that of the American people in government. In spite of such defection Asbury remained a dictator and moulded the form of church organization on the principles in which he believed. At minor points he had to give way, but American Methodism owes much of its system to his moulding in the formative days. Everybody respected Asbury because his discipline of himself was as severe as of the clergy over whom he ruled with an iron hand.

Francis Asbury is only a conspicuous member of a great host of frontier evangelists who moved like flaming torches through the American wilderness. Usually on horseback but sometimes on foot they went from clearing to clearing, carrying the Christian message of good-will, challenging men and women to own their responsibility to live right lives in whatever circumstances they might find themselves. The missionaries were usually single men, paid a pittance for a salary, but as consecrated to their Protestant service as ever a Jesuit or a Benedictine monk. They kept pace with the advancing frontier, moving from the Alleghanies to the Rockies as settlement progressed, succeeding one another as men sickened and died, but always with the same spirit of devotion, and with the same gospel of personal salvation for men lost in sin.

Home missions on the American frontier make up a thrilling story. They belong to the age that gave this nation birth and adolescence. The frontier has disappeared and with it the old scenes have passed and the flavour of adventure is no more. But new tasks have come to the old societies that were organized to carry on evangelism. The handicapped races are later recipients of home mission endeavour. Indians, Negroes, our Latin American wards, the immigrants from Europe who throng our great cities—these constitute the main field of home mission enterprise today. But still in the sparsely settled regions of the great West, where great plains stretch away to the horizon and snow-capped peaks melt into the sky people gather to listen to the missionary, and mission boards aid in the building of little churches.

Religion has combined with those sturdy qualities that the frontier produced to make a virile type of western manhood. Whether in Church or State it is independent, masterful, courageous. It stands for freedom and democracy with the intensity of pioneers in the East, like Roger Williams and Alexander Campbell. These qualities had the deficiencies of their virtues. Individualism bred religious rivalries, and churches of various names competed disastrously for local supremacy. Self-reliance sometimes produced a cocksureness that would not brook differences of theology or political opinion, but on the whole the West has outdone the East in its progressiveness and strength of purpose to achieve.

Francis Asbury and others of his kind were builders of a church and a nation. They saw that religion was needed to make the nation strong. Masterful or democratic they made their contribution to the future, and that future is reaping the harvest of their labours. Asbury believed in the future of America. He had visions of prairies dotted with farms and villages. On his far journeys through river valleys and over rugged mountains he meditated on earthly scenes as well as heavenly expectations. And because such men had the visions they helped to turn vision into reality. America would have been built if they had not lived; without them it would not have been reared on solid foundations without which a great nation cannot endure.

12

JOHN FREDERICK OBERLIN

IN a hill village among the Vosges mountains of eastern France is a house that was built a hundred and fifty years ago and occupied by a unique representative of Protestantism. The village of Waldbach is located in the blue Alsatian mountains about which so many amateur musicians have sung. It was a small collection of houses grouped around a church, not very different from many other towns in similar locations. It had had ordinary ministers of the parish, who conducted the proper religious services, but had no vision of a larger ministry for their rural folk until Oberlin came.

John Frederick Oberlin was born in 1740 in Strassburg. The city was a part of that debatable ground of Alsace which at various times in history has been tossed back and forth, like a football of international politics, between France and Germany. After the Thirty Years' War of the seventeenth century Alsace was French until the Franco-Prussian War of 1870. Large numbers of the people were of German origin, but during the long period of French possession they became real Frenchmen in their sympathies. When Oberlin was born the French and the Germans were entering upon one of their international contests, the War of the Austrian Succession, which was to add to the border territory of France. It was a war which had a long reach, for Englishmen entered the contest against France, and English colonists in America felt the hostility of Canadian French and their Indian allies in those dreadful raids that brought torture and death so often to the frontier settlements.

In the year of Oberlin's birth Jonathan Edwards was located still in the frontier town of Northampton. George Whitefield was making his journey of evangelism along the Atlantic coast of North America. John Wesley was starting upon his daring venture of outdoor preaching to the working people of England. These events did not travel as news to Strassburg or to the mountain village of Waldbach in the Ban de la Roche. Oberlin himself was unheralded as a child who was to be remembered in both Europe and America.

The city of Strassburg was a centre of education as well as of population. The child's father was a teacher in a school preparatory to the university, and an older brother was a professor in the university. The mother was daughter of another professor, and she was a woman of rare gifts of personality. Born with such a heritage, and with the limitations to indulgence that are imposed by the small income of a teacher, the boy John grew up to value character and attainment more than money. He was conscientiously studious, doggedly persistent in carrying through whatever he undertook, and he stuck to his university discipline until he had obtained the degree of doctor of philosophy, an indication that he was fitted to become an educator. But that was not to be his career.

To please his mother the son accompanied her to

church, and after a time decided upon the profession of minister in a Lutheran church rather than upon a professorship. The Lutheran standards did not require a deeply religious spirit as a qualification for the pulpit, but Oberlin was willing to devote his life to a humble service of God's people wherever he might find the way opening before him, and he was disposed to take a small parish as a means of preparation for a larger one, in the same spirit of thoroughness that characterized his university career.

While he was waiting for an opening he was in Strassburg, acting as tutor in the family of a surgeon, and he improved the opportunity to study medicine and surgery, as might a missionary who expected to find such knowledge useful among pagan and uncivilized peoples. Botany was another subject that interested him and seemed useful.

Still uncertain of his future, Oberlin presently accepted an opportunity to join the French army as a chaplain. He had a liking for the military. He had played at soldiering when a boy, and enjoyed the drills which his father practised with his growing boys. He believed, too, that he could be useful to the young men in the army. But before he could get started in the routine duties of his position, he was visited by a parish minister from the hills and summoned to go to that district as a pastor, with the same urgency that Farel used to persuade Calvin to man the post at Geneva a hundred and thirty years before.

It was a summons to heroism. It meant that Oberlin must become pastor of a struggling parish of five

country villages in a district of country that was as
backward as Ireland in its misery and squalor a hundred years ago. The people were poor in purse, list-
less in temper, discouraged and unambitious. They
lived without the comforts of life, housed in miserable
huts, with little to eat or wear. Winter chilled them
for long months of the year, and the short summer
barely ripened the unimproved fruits and scanty crops.
Each village was isolated, without roads over which
the people might get to know and help one another.

Oberlin was attracted to the parish as an opportunity for service, though he foresaw discouragement,
poverty, and possible hardship. He made the decision
to go as soon as he could be relieved of his obligation
to the army, and in 1767, when twenty-seven years of
age, he arrived in the highlands. The village of Waldbach was three thousand feet above sea level; others
of the villages were higher up. The heights of the
Vosges were higher still. The people were shut off
from the sunny plains of France on the west, and open
to icy blasts from the north. It was not an easy
country in which to live and labour. But Oberlin was
happy from the outset in anticipation of his opportunity to serve his folk among the hills.

The situation was not entirely hopeless. Oberlin's
predecessor was a man of education and imagination.
He had opened schools and provided musical training
for the young people. He had prepared a catechism
that they might understand the real meaning of religion. But he had generations of indifference to over-
come and he did not get far. It was Oberlin's task to

pick up his activities and carry them farther. Fortunately for his strength and poise of spirit he loved nature. When his heart ached at the poverty and ignorance and suffering of his people, he loved to gaze upon the summits and rest his faith there. He was susceptible to the beauty of the scenes before him whether in their rich green or in their robes of snow. He had faith to believe that the God who had made the world beautiful would not be content with an unbeautiful race of men. And it was his task to mould into beauty the lives and characters of the men and women and children who inhabited those hills.

Oberlin belongs among the pathfinders of Christian history, because he had the insight to perceive that he must blaze new trails in applying Christianity to rural churches. In a remarkable way he anticipated methods and ideas that only now are being accepted as reasonable. He saw the importance of religious education. He caught the truth that religion should be a part of man's whole life and personality, a thing for every day and all the work and play of the day. He mapped out his task in a large way, planning for bodies and minds as well as spirits, for the community as a whole as well as for the individuals in it.

Oberlin never conceived his mission in the large way of John Wesley. He had no ambition to travel all over Alsace, and even France, preaching the gospel of repentance and faith. He had not the gifts of an evangelist, or a conviction that that was his work. He was no revivalist like Jonathan Edwards to frighten men as a means of making them religious. Nor was he

a reformer like Luther, or an apostle of freedom like
Roger Williams. Each of these men had his own task
and his contribution to make. Oberlin's ambition was
to cultivate a human desert in the midst of the mountains, and make the desert blossom with growing beau-
ties of character and improving aspects of environment.

A primary element in his purpose was to improve
education. Oberlin had sense enough to know that
good schools meant equipment, curriculum, and teachers. He knew that he could not depend on his own
people to raise money for education. They were very
poor; feudal burdens still remained in rural France,
and taxes were heavy. His own salary was only a
thousand francs a year. From friends in Strassburg
he secured enough money to insure a building in Waldbach, and then he began to plan for another village.
Meantime he was looking for teachers. He knew how
important it was to find the right kind. They must be
willing to work for a small salary, they must be sympathetic with the community, and they must be patient
in trying to improve local conditions.

Oberlin had novel ideas about courses of instruction.
He tried kindergarten methods in the primary grade,
and employed two women, one to direct the handwork,
the other to direct recreation, for Oberlin did not believe that mental discipline was the whole of education. From the beginning and through all the grades
ran instruction in religion, and to teach self-control he
introduced student government into the higher grades,
experimenting even with the primary pupils. The ele-

ments of botany, physics, and astronomy, the study of
nature and art, and lessons in health, were all a part
of a curriculum that sounds so modern that it is almost
unbelievable that Oberlin should have thought of these
matters, much less have introduced them successfully.

Such unconventional methods of training children
aroused the distrust and antagonism of the people.
They feared that schools would mean more taxes.
They did not like the direct way in which the minister
presented his ideas and intentions. Some of them
planned to seize him and punish him, but he dared
them to do it and they slunk away ashamed. He converted them to his ideas finally by the proven cor-
rectness of his methods and by the sheer strength of
his will. He attended to all the details of superintendence himself, and he won out. His educational efforts
included the preparation of text-books for his own villages, and he published an annual almanac which contained space for a diary and lists of names suitable for
children. Nothing that could help his people was overlooked, including a circulating library. His initial successes encouraged his Strassburg friends to increase
their subscriptions, and the hardest part of his enterprise was over during the first four years.

At first a sister made a home for the parson, but he
married in 1768. His wife was an orphan, the daughter of a former professor in the University of Strassburg. She possessed qualities that fitted the needs of
Oberlin's nature, and proved a dependable help to him
in his parish plans.

Oberlin saw that he could not hope to improve living conditions and arouse the social interest of the village people without good roads. These would make visiting possible and awaken the interest of the people in the world outside their own hamlet, and would make possible the exportation of surplus products from field and farm. His people were too prejudiced to fall in with his plans, and they thought that he should be made to stick to his business of preaching religion conventionally instead of applying it to secular matters, but he insisted upon building a road, and when they balked he commenced operations almost alone. Cheerfully he drove his pick into the ground, vigorously he plied his spade. Shame drove others to join him. More and more came, and he showed his executive ability in telling them what to do and getting the work done. He used the same method in bridge building.

Seven years of such pioneer service gave Oberlin a reputation, and he was invited to go to America to take the leadership of an immigrant settlement of Swiss in Pennsylvania. He felt that it was a call to service that could not be refused, and he hoped that his Vosges parishioners would be interested to carry on the enterprises that he had planted. He was on the point of going to America when the Revolutionary War broke out, upsetting his plans and making his proposed program for the new settlement impracticable, for a time at least. He refused other tempting invitations, and stayed at his post. The death of his wife only drove him into harder work, that he might do her part as well as his own, and it never became feasible to go to America.

He preached the gospel of Jesus to love God and one's neighbour, and then he practised that gospel to the best of his ability. He found charity always necessary, but he organized it so that it would not pauperize. He was always hunting for the causes, and trying to go to the root of every man's problem. He saw that poverty could be lessened greatly if agriculture could be improved, and this became one of his chief interests. As with the schools, he gave farming his careful attention. He investigated the soil to find what it could produce best, encouraged the wider cultivation of the potato and other unusual vegetables, and organized agricultural clubs to spread a knowledge of the newer methods. New seed for grain culture, better fertilizers, the introduction of irrigation where it was needed and of drainage where opposite conditions prevailed, marked his wisdom and common sense and indefatigable industry.

Nothing escaped him. When necessary he loaned money out of his few savings that his people might buy machinery or better breeds of cattle. He was on the watch continually for improvements of all kinds. Obtaining cuttings from the best fruit trees he started a nursery, secured the distribution of better orchard trees, and organized a horticultural society to make permanent these gains. He broke down the hostility of his enemies, converted the skeptical to believe that he knew practical farming, and through everything kept his spirit of optimism and enthusiasm.

When the French Revolution came Oberlin and his people were drawn into the conflict. They delighted in their escape from feudalism. He tried to keep the religious sanctions of life. Amid the changes that took place he remained the community leader, and when religion was abolished he was elected public orator and discussed public and private virtues. He hoped that true liberty would not fail, but he had no sympathy with the Terror. The shrinkage of his income made living circumscribed and much of his charity impossible. The scanty living weakened him physically, but he survived. At the end of the Terror he took private pupils into his home, and resumed his ministry, declining a salary.

At the age of fifty-six Oberlin had made a wide reputation, and he was invited to a parish with greater opportunities. But he refused, saying that it would take him ten years more to carry out his plans and ten more to correct mistakes. He lived with service as his first thought in all that he undertook to do. Realizing the need of the circulation of the Christian Scriptures, he welcomed the organization of the British and Foreign Bible Society, formed an auxiliary society in his own district, and took care to see that his people had the Bible at home. He continued his social ministries, never forgetting that religion was to be applied to every-day life. In recognition of his unusual service to the mountain region in which he had worked for more than fifty years he was given the medal of the Legion of Honour by the king of France. With customary humility he said: What have I done to deserve it? The National Agricultural Society of Paris also bestowed upon him a gold medal in appreciation

of his efforts to improve the agriculture of his parishioners.

Oberlin lived to a ripe old age, preserving the spirit
of youth and serving his folk in ways that opened to
him. When he could no longer preach, he sent messages through the printing press, and prayed for the
names on the parish register. In the spring of 1826
his long life came to a worthy end, like a shock of corn
in full maturity. Protestants and Catholics alike followed him to his grave and helped to lay away his
body. His spirit of service crossed the Atlantic Ocean
and is perpetuated in Oberlin College, friend of the
oppressed and light of liberty as well as learning in the
heart of America.

13

WILLIAM CAREY

WHILE Oberlin was a private tutor in Strassburg and Wesley was riding on circuit
across the shires of England, William Carey
was born in the midland county of Northampton.
The spirit of devotion to Christian duty which characterized both Oberlin and Wesley was to drive him
to the other side of the world as a missionary to India.
It was to make him constant to his purpose even in
the midst of the gravest difficulties. Carey was to become known as the pioneer of those organized efforts
that have had as their objective the conversion of a
pagan world to Christianity. He started life with
small advantages. He was not a minister's or professor's son. He enjoyed no university education. The
world was not ready to welcome him into the ranks of
leadership. He forged to the front because he felt
within him an urge to duty, as great as the soldier feels
in the face of the enemy, and because he was faithful
he became great.

When William Carey was born Oberlin's France was
at war with Wesley's England. The Seven Years'
War was desolating Europe, and carrying distress to
countries as far apart as Canada and India. It ended
soon with the defeat of France and the transfer of
those far-sundered lands to English control. The
French had exploited Canada, but they did not colonize

it adequately. Now the valley of the Saint Lawrence was to be added to the Atlantic coast colonies of Great Britain. In India France and England both had established their trading posts in the midst of a swarming population of potential customers, and both were eager for exclusive trading rights. They left the case to the arbitrament of war and England won. Henceforth her traders were in the ascendant, and her empire slowly expanded.

Carey was born at Paulerspury, where his father was a weaver. It was the year 1761. When he was six years old his father obtained the office of schoolmaster and parish clerk, a position that his own father had occupied, and in his father's school the boy William learned the rudiments of his education. More important in turning his mind to an adventuresome disposition was his uncle, Peter Carey, who had been in Canada during the war. In the Carey home uncle and nephew were absorbed more than once in tales of Indians and the frontier, and both delighted in the descriptions of New World forests and lakes, as they loved the fair countryside of England. Together they worked in the garden and the boy laid the foundations of the botanical knowledge for which he has become famous.

When William was fourteen he began to earn his own living in the fields, but soon became apprenticed to a shoemaker in a neighbouring village. Those were the years when the American colonies south of Canada were in revolt against Great Britain, and William Carey was thrilled by the recital of events in his shop and in the village. But he had other things to think of. He was troubled about the state of his soul. He tried to find satisfaction in the parish churches, but after he had obtained peace of mind by centering his trust on the teaching of the Bible he joined the fortunes of a small dissenting church. Meantime his studious inclinations and a chance discovery of a Greek commentary on the New Testament interested him in language study. After a few years Carey's master died, and presently he took over the business and married into the family.

During those years of finding himself Carey gave no promise of becoming an outstanding man. He worked at his trade, dug in his garden, worshipped in the little chapel, and sometimes spoke to the edification of others, but no one could have dreamed of his future. That which stirred him as nothing else had and gave him a zest for missionary service was the reading of an account of Captain Cook's Voyages in the South Seas. The explorer saw only the glamour of the adventure; Carey saw the possibility of transforming heathen savages into civilized Christians. It seemed hopelessly visionary for a journeyman shoemaker to cherish an ambition that he might become a missionary to the islands of the far Pacific, but such dreams are the stuff of which achievement is wrought.

Not yet was Carey an ordained minister. He had been immersed and associated himself with Baptists. He had preached occasionally to such small churches as wished to listen to him. In 1785 he was ordained. During all this time he followed his trade, adding to

it instruction in an evening school to those who felt
the need. Before long he became pastor of a rural
Baptist church at a salary of a few pounds a year,
supplementing his earnings by his trade. He enjoyed
the friendship of the other Baptist ministers in the
association of churches to which he belonged, and he
talked missions to them, though they were skeptical
about the practicability of any such undertaking. The
missionary idea had been implanted in the ancient
Church. Catholic monks toured Europe in the Middle
Ages, and Jesuits and Franciscans carried the cross
among the natives of America. But except for a few
individuals, chiefly Moravians, Protestants had produced no missionary movement, organized and effective. To think that a poor company of Baptists in
England could evangelize even one pagan island seemed
a crazy idea.

While the missionary idea was simmering in his
mind, Carey was called to a better church. The
Harvey Lane congregation in Leicester invited him
from the country to the town. He studied hard to
fit himself for his task and he preached heart-searching
sermons to his people. His evangelistic fervour drove
him out of town to preach in the neighbouring villages,
and he organized churches out of his converts. If he
could not find a way to go to the South Sea, he could
be a home missionary in England. Soon after he went
to Leicester he was made secretary of the Nonconformist committee that was working to secure the re-
peal of the intolerant acts of earlier Parliaments. He
rejoiced in the beginnings of the French Revolution.

Like a true Baptist, he loved freedom. He joined a coterie of students of the sciences, and learned more about nature than he ever knew before. He did not disdain to pick up knowledge among friends and acquaintances, as he did in his cobbler's shop.

It was in 1792 that he published "the charter of modern missions." It was a pamphlet of eighty-seven pages with the burdensome title of " Enquiry into the Obligations of Christians to use Means for the Conversion of the Heathens; in which the Religious State of the Different Nations of the World, the Success of Former Undertakings, and the Practicability of Further Undertakings are Considered." It contained a fund of information and proved an epoch-making work in the history of Christian missions. In May of the same year he preached a sermon in the Baptist chapel in Nottingham, where the Northampton Association of churches met. He took as his text: " Enlarge the place of thy tent, and let them stretch forth the curtains of thine habitations. Spare not, lengthen thy cords and strengthen thy stakes. . . . Thy seed shall inherit the Gentiles." The theme of the sermon was: " Expect great things from God. Attempt great things for God." In the delivery of the sermon Carey gave expression to the beliefs and hopes that had animated him for years, and he lighted " a burning bush of missionary revelation " that has never gone out. Afterward the ministers deliberated whether they could do anything for foreign missions. They were poor and they doubted, good Calvinists that they were, whether it was their obligation. Dr.

Ryland, who had baptized Carey and was his good
friend, commanded him to remember that if God
wanted to convert the heathen He could do it without
the help of either of them. But Carey's importunity
won over Andrew Fuller to his way of thinking, and
Andrew Fuller moved the preparation of a missionary plan for the next ministers' meeting, and it was
carried.

Andrew Fuller was the Baptist minister at Ketter-
ing. There in October the meeting met that was to
go down into history as the birthplace of modern missions. Several of the ministers present had not heard
Carey's sermon and they were timid. But enough
stood with Carey to carry the meeting, and a resolu-
tion was adopted which read: "Humbly desirous of
making an effort for the propagation of the Gospel
amongst the heathen, according to the recommenda-
tions of Carey's 'Enquiry,' we unanimously resolve
to act in Society together for this purpose; and, as
in the divided state of Christendom each denomination, by exerting itself separately, seems likeliest to
accomplish the great end, we name this the Particular
Baptist Society for the Propagation of the Gospel
amongst the Heathen." Then twelve ministers sub-
scribed about thirteen pounds to initiate the task of
saving the world. Carey offered himself as the first
missionary.

Carey was eager to go as a missionary himself. His
preference was for the island of Tahiti in the Pacific
Ocean as an objective point, but the attention of the
Society was attracted to India by an independent

medical missionary, John Thomas, who had been living there, and the Society undertook to send both Thomas and Carey to India as its representatives. After discouraging delays Carey and his family started their voyage on a sailing ship. It was a long and tiresome journey of five months, and during that time no landing was made. The family reached Calcutta in 1793.

The Society had underestimated the expense of getting a mission started, Calcutta was an expensive place to live in, and before long the Careys were in danger of starvation. After seven months Carey was forced to accept a secular position in an indigo factory at Mudnabati, north of the great city. There for five years he served as superintendent, and spent his spare time in preparation for the missionary opportunity that he expected would come to him. He mastered the Bengali tongue with comparative ease, for he had a natural gift for languages. He set up a printing press, and he preached to the people as he had opportunity. His love of nature made him delight to go on his business errands through rural Bengal, and he became well acquainted with its fauna and flora. His occupation gave him the opportunity for self-support that he believed in as the proper method of conducting a mission, and thrift made the undertaking prosperous.

After six years reinforcements came from England and a mission station was opened at Serampore, a Danish trading station. The English East India Company which controlled Calcutta was concerned selfishly with profits alone, and missionaries were not trading assets. The council even objected to missionary passengers on its ships, so that when Robert Morrison of England wished to go to China on a Christian mission he had to sail to America and transship there.

At Serampore a large building was purchased and made into a common home for the three missionary families. They formed a Christian brotherhood, ate their meals in common, and saved money which they put into a common purse. The ideals of Carey looking to self-support were realized. This made it possible for the Society at home to use its funds elsewhere, and the success of the Serampore mission greatly assisted in encouraging similar undertakings.

Carey and his associates appreciated the desirability of starting the mission on a broad foundation. They pushed out their outstations by means of evangelizing efforts, and they planned schools. With characteristic breadth of vision Carey saw the important place that education must have in the development of Christian civilization in the East. He saw that native Christian leaders must be trained, for he was wise enough to see that English missions would never be able to instruct the whole of India. He interested himself in schools of all grades, and founded a Christian college at Serampore. An important feature of the work of the early missions was to translate the Bible and other religious books into the language of the people. Carey had completed a Bengali New Testament about the time he had settled at Serampore, and he continued his linguistic activities by translating into other dialects. By the time of Carey's death the Bible had been put into forty dialects of central and southern

Asia through the labours of Carey and others. He published a newspaper in the vernacular.

The conditions of living in India were trying to a European. The climate was hot; the people were neither attractive nor teachable; food, customs, language, were all strange. Distance from country and friends was depressing, and ill health was frequently a burden. Mrs. Carey was a victim of permanent depression, a circumstance that added heavily to her husband's responsibilities. Few persons showed any interest in a foreign religion, and public opinion threatened to ostracize any who should join the mission. The first convert was a carpenter, Krishna Pal. He became the author of a hymn for the communion service, which is often sung in English-speaking churches. The first stanza is as follows:

> "O thou, my soul, forget no more
> The Friend who all thy misery bore.
> Let every idol be forgot,
> But O my soul, forget Him not."

Since the principle of self-support was accepted, it was necessary for Carey to earn a living for his family. The Bengali New Testament translation gave him a reputation, and he was surprised one day to be offered a professorship of Bengali in the Fort William College which had been founded as a training school for English officials. Though distrustful of his ability, Carey accepted the post, and later his professorship was enlarged to include the Mahratta and Sanscrit languages. Carey received a salary of fifteen hundred pounds a year, but most of it he turned over to the work of the mission. He did not give all his time to education. Meantime his colleague Marshman was taking in fees to the amount of a thousand pounds a year from a boarding school, most of which he gave to the mission. In those ways a fund was accumulated which made possible generous missionary activities in the years to come. Carey held his position for more than twenty years.

Carey's interests were many. He enjoyed his garden, and he became an authority in oriental horticulture. He established a hospital for lepers. He helped to abolish certain cruelties, such as the practice of burning widows, many of whom were children in age, on the funeral pyres of their dead husbands. Another horrible custom was the sacrifice of children to the god of the river Ganges. Carey was commissioned to inquire into the practice, and his report secured the abolition of the custom. Another of his philanthropic interests was a school which he founded for the children of poor parents. With all the rest Carey found time to preach and to share the responsibilities of the whole mission.

It was a great encouragement to the English Baptist mission when the English Parliament, in granting a new charter to the East India Company, insisted that missionaries should be permitted to land and work anywhere in India. The law made possible the coming of new missionaries. Other missionary organizations had followed the Baptist pioneering. The London Missionary Society of Nonconformists and the

Church Missionary Society of Anglicans had been founded, and the former established a south of India mission in 1804. After the new law was passed English Episcopalians and Methodists and American Congregationalists and Baptists pressed into the country. American Baptists had been interested in Carey and had contributed to his mission. Later they adopted Adoniram Judson, who had started for India as a missionary of the Congregationalist American Board, the first of American foreign missionary societies.

Besides the opposition of the Company, other serious obstacles lay in the way of missionary success from the beginning, and these were not removed with the end of official opposition. Caste was a continual hindrance. The high caste people would not mingle with the low caste folk, and converts were reluctant to abolish caste distinctions. Sympathy was established most easily between the missionaries and the outcasts who ranked at the bottom of the social scale, and the first Christian mass movements began with them. Yet there were favourable circumstances as the years passed. Western civilization was gaining among the people. English rule was constantly gaining prestige and extending its authority. The later missionaries had the advantage over the pioneers in the linguistic studies and the evangelistic experience. The time demanded men of ability, of breadth of view, of thoughtful insight, of patient courage. Such a man was William Carey. The success of the mission that he planted encouraged missionary enterprises in many other lands.

In spite of trials with the home board and with

younger missionaries, with family afflictions, and personal illness, William Carey grew old cheerfully and filled the days full of occupation with an energy uncommon enough in India. His last years were years of peace. He gave more than forty years to India, dying at last at Serampore in 1834. By that time Government was friendly and harmony had been restored in mission circles. The mission had extended out far into the country. The educational work of the mission had been endowed and had prospered. And the world seemed a better place to live in than it had been when Carey landed in India. He had lived a worthy life and his end was peace.

The missionary enterprise launched by the small group of English ministers inspired by Carey has extended until it has gone around the world. Christians of every communion have vied with one another to extend missionary activities. In education, evangelism, medical service, Bible translation, philanthropy, and industrial training, missionaries have given unstinted service to races steeped in decayed civilizations or in savagery. Missionaries are heroes and sometimes martyrs. They expect to face perils and to endure hardships. They are made of pioneer stuff. They are moved by the Spirit of God and they are builders of His kingdom. William Carey was but the first of many who have gone out as representatives of Christendom to win the pagan world for Christ.

14

ALEXANDER CAMPBELL

DURING the time when William Carey was finding his way to the hearts of the people of India, a boy was born in Ireland who was to carry a message to the West. He was not Irish by race, for his family was Scotch on his father's side and French Huguenot on his mother's. But both of his parents were residents of Ireland, and out in the countryside of County Antrim he was born in 1788. His father, Thomas Campbell, was a Presbyterian minister. The boy went to the village school, and supplemented his schooling in his father's study. He was very fond of sports, and during his growing years he played and worked on the farm harder than he studied. In Scotland religion and education have gone hand in hand, and a minister readily turns his hand to teaching. For a time Thomas Campbell conducted an academy, and Alexander learned how to teach as his father's associate. While still a youth he joined the Presbyterian church, and planned to give his life to the Christian ministry.

In those days many English families were emigrating to America. Thousands of Scotch-Irish found homes in the western counties of Pennsylvania, Virginia, and the Carolinas. Some of their descendants still live among the Southern mountains, and preserve the old traits of the race. Thomas Campbell was among those who saw a better future for his growing family in America, and since his health was not good and his physician advised a sea voyage he crossed to America and settled in western Pennsylvania. There he preached to a group of Presbyterians like himself, Seceders by name, because they had separated from the regularly established Church of Scotland. As the family of a pioneering emigrant follows him to the United States from Europe in these days, so the Campbells started from Ireland, but sickness and shipwreck delayed them.

Alexander improved the opportunity to attend classes in the University of Glasgow for a year, and in 1809 the family set sail in his charge for the New World. When they arrived at their American port, they found that it was a long, tedious journey to their destination, but Alexander was cheerful and fond of nature and there was much to see along the way. The village of Washington in Pennsylvania where Thomas Campbell had located is now a railroad junction southwest of the city of Pittsburgh. Then it was a small settlement of a few hundred persons. Many of them lived in rude log houses. It was a rolling country rich in fertile soil and pasture, but the hillsides were forest-clothed, and people were only beginning to improve the rich farming land.

When Alexander arrived he found his father in trouble with his Seceding congregation because he favoured Christian communion with all denominational groups. This experience, put alongside sectarian disturbances with which they had been connected in the old country, made both father and son incline to independency in religion, and to an emphasis upon the primitive Christianity common to all believers. Competitive denominationalism in America was widespread and relentless, and the Campbells were presently leading a movement of religious reform based on the simple teachings of the Bible and the principle of Christian unity.

This movement crystallized in the organization of the Christian Association of Washington in 1809. This was designed to bring together those persons who were sympathetic with the principles for which the Association stood, and it was hoped that similar organizations might be centres of ferment for the ideas of the Campbells. Alexander Campbell faced the question of his life-work, and resolved to give his best efforts to furthering the movement that had been begun. He gave long hours to study for the further training of a mind that had not been highly educated, and he developed qualities of leadership. He had the gift of public speech and a fine presence on the platform. He was not afraid to meet any man in debate, and in the years that followed his discussions were many. He was sure of his own ground, skilful in argument and rebuttal, with a gift for sarcasm when it was an aid, and he regularly discomfited those who were pitted against him. It was an age which relished were pitted against him. It was an age which relished the excitement of physical contest, and Campbell won popularity and fame from his numerous wordy encounters.

Among his principal contests was a debate with a Presbyterian minister of Ohio on the subject of baptism. Baptists were increasing in the region and the subjects of infant baptism and immersion were favourite topics of discussion. Later he debated on the same subject with another Presbyterian champion. He was rash enough to take issue with a Catholic archbishop on the question of the infallibility of the pope. His best known debate was with Robert Owen, the English manufacturer and philanthropist. Owen was an unbeliever of the truth of Christianity in an unskeptical age, but he debated with more courtesy than the denominational champions.

These debates extending over a period of years gave Alexander Campbell a wide reputation, but not until he had served a local apprenticeship as a minister. He ventured to preach his first sermon in a grove in 1810. He was still a part of the Washington group of independents. About the same time the Association became a church, which from its location is known as the Brush Run church. The members of the Association had found themselves uncomfortable elsewhere. The elder Campbell was pastor of the church, and Alexander was its licensed preacher.

In 1812 he married Margaret Brown, the daughter of a farmer living over the Pennsylvania border in that neck of West Virginia which is between the Ohio River and the western boundary line of Pennsylvania. He made his home on the Brown farm and spent much of his time on the work of the farm, preaching here and there as he had opportunity. The Campbells were literal interpreters of the Bible, and when Alexander became a father he looked for Scriptural authority for the baptism of his child. He could not find it and he became dissatisfied with his own baptism. He was therefore immersed by a Baptist minister, and others of his own family and church followed his example. In most respects Campbell was now a Baptist, and it was not long before the Brush Run church became a member of the Redstone Association of Baptist churches.

Alexander Campbell was pastor of the Brush Run church after his father moved to Ohio, and he preached frequently in other Baptist churches. But the denominational spirit was strong, and doctrinal issues were finely spun. Campbell was out of sympathy with denominationalism, and was not a stern enough Calvinist to satisfy the Baptists. He was inclined, too, to emphasize the differences between them. In his own village of Bethany, West Virginia, he founded Buffalo Seminary to educate the local young people, and to attract young men who could be trained to preach his opinions. This institution was discontinued after a few years, but he did not lose his liking for an educational occupation.

He had written locally for the press, and in 1823 he started the *Christian Baptist* to broadcast his opinions. His success decided him to continue the periodical, and he developed a profitable printing business which widely extended his influence for decades. Within a few years he changed the *Christian Baptist* to the *Millennial Harbinger,* when he concluded that Christ would return soon for His millennial reign. Though he mistook the date, his periodical had a wide circulation. He was as outspoken in the columns of his paper as on the public platform, and his criticism of denominational organizations from Sunday schools to foreign missions angered the ministers of many churches.

It was becoming clear that Baptists and Campbellites, or Disciples, as Campbell preferred to call his followers, could not get on in the same churches, even in that sparsely settled neck of the woods. By 1827 Baptist Associations were excluding churches of Disciples, and Alexander Campbell saved himself from expulsion only by withdrawing with some of his church from the Brush Run church, and joining another Baptist Association. From that time the Disciples were virtually a new denomination, though few in numbers. Baptists and Disciples agreed on the New Testament basis of the Church and on baptism, and so were much nearer together than with Presbyterians or Methodists, but on minor points there was much friction.

Campbell's unremitting study of the Bible made him a master of its contents and familiar with its language. He liked certain private translations that had been made, and thinking that some simplification of expression would help to a better understanding he made a translation of the New Testament which was published in 1827. At a later time he was a firm supporter of the American Bible Union, which had been organized by the Baptists who were not satisfied with the usual translation of the Greek word for baptize. For the

Union he subsequently made a new version of the book
of Acts. Because most hymn-books contained so many
hymns that were not in harmony with his understanding of biblical teaching, he eliminated most of them
and published a selection of about one hundred and
twenty-five hymns for the use of the Disciples. His
publishing interests seemed reason enough for the establishment of a government post-office for him, of
which he was postmaster.

Though in his Bethany home he lived far from the
madding crowd, Campbell liked to travel, and the increasing demands for his services sent him in all directions. He gave over some of his editorial work in
order to have more freedom to travel. He had a growing family of daughters, but he did not find it necessary to remain at home on account of family cares.
He was made a delegate to a constitutional convention
of the state of Virginia, for he was living in a section
that was then within the western counties of the Old
Dominion. He was popular in Kentucky, especially in
Lexington, where Transylvania College was located,
and he went frequently into that district. Several
times he went south of Virginia, once to New Orleans.
On one occasion he travelled to Missouri, then a part
of the Far West. He was a welcome visitor to New
York and Philadelphia. Once he went to Washington
to accept an invitation to make an address before the
assembled houses of Congress. It is interesting to
think of him surmounting the difficulties of travel,
which in certain sections of country were annoying, and
coming into contact with thousands of people who al-

ways were impressed with his strong personality. He craved acquaintance and the stir of crowds, though he loved the country. He was at his best before an audience, whether preaching a sermon or debating a proposition. He had a tall, athletic figure, was self-reliant in his attitude, and ready with humour and good cheer. He gave an impression of intellectual ability, with his broad brow crowned with coal-black hair, and the impression was not lost when he spoke. Alexander Campbell must be recognized as a man of mark in a time when his own section of country did not lack for prominent men, even along the frontier.

Added strength came to the Disciples in a union of many Christians with their body. The Christian Connection is a combination of three distinct groups of independents who came out of larger denominations about the end of the eighteenth century. One of these groups resulted from dissatisfaction among some of the Methodists in 1793 under the leadership of James O'Kelley. A second group was a secession from the Baptists in northern New England, and a third was from the Presbyterians. This last was due to opposition shown by the Presbyterian leaders to revival methods. Its leader was Barton W. Stone. All these groups cared less for the shibboleths of denominations than for the simple and urgent gospel of Jesus.

In their principles there was not much difference between the Disciples and the Christians. It was mainly a matter of emphasis. The Christians appealed more directly to the emotions and the will by means of evangelistic methods, and made rapid gains in the number of their adherents. They cared nothing for denominational loyalty but much for Christian unity. The Disciples put their emphasis on the Bible. Nothing of Bible teaching should be neglected or altered; nothing that did not have Scriptural sanction was authoritative in religion. In his literal interpretation Campbell sometimes lost sight of the general in the particular and sometimes misinterpreted. But the close similarity between Disciples and Christians made their coalescence easy, and the union of forces was general in Ohio, Kentucky, and Tennessee, but each denomination still persists.

Campbell did a great service to the frontier churches of America when he went back to first principles. Baptists and Presbyterians and Methodists were overstressing their differences, fighting wordy battles over points of theology and church ordinances. They all claimed to get their authority from the Bible, but their interpretations did not agree. It was wholesome to get back of denominationalism to a common Christianity as Jesus interpreted it. Alexander Campbell had his own peculiar ideas about baptism, believing that remission of sin was not complete until baptism released, so to speak, the forgiving grace of God, differing in this opinion from both Baptists and non-Baptists. He was militant in his advocacy of his own ideas. And he brought into existence a new denomination, contrary as that was to his purpose. But in his loyalty to the Bible he was the most consistent of the Bible interpreters of his time, and in his advocacy of church unity he was a century ahead of his own age.

As he grew older he was impressed anew with the importance of education. In 1840 he renewed his effort to secure an institution which would provide a trained ministry for the Disciples. In his own West Virginia community he established Bethany College and shortly assumed the presidency. He travelled about to get funds for its support, but when at home he gave diligent attention to the work of teaching. It might be said of him as it was of another, that instead of a chair he had a settee, for he included in his portfolio of specialties biblical instruction and lectures on political economy and mental and moral philosophy.

On public questions he was less dogmatic than on religion. The controversy over slavery grew more heated in his late years until Civil War broke out. Campbell took the position that slavery was an inexpedient method of industry for the South to employ in the days of nineteenth century civilization, but to him there was no great moral wrong in the relation of master and servant that required a crusade. While such a position aroused no enthusiasm, it kept the peace at a time when denominations were breaking apart over the question.

Campbell was proud of the gains that his opinions made outside of the United States. They found their way to Canada and to Great Britain. He himself went on a visit to each of these countries. It was in 1847 that he crossed the ocean. He was invited to preach on shipboard, and in England he was welcomed in a number of cities. He spoke in London, but Disciples

were few and he was not well advertised. Crossing
the Channel, he made a visit to Paris. In Scotland he
spoke and lectured in Edinburgh and other places.
Unfortunately opposition developed to his opinions,
and his opponents stirred up feeling against him on
the slavery question. Soon a Presbyterian minister
sued him for damages on account of certain remarks
which Campbell had made. Refusing bail, Campbell
went to prison, and for ten days he had a taste of
English inhospitality, but friends visited him continually and letters of sympathy poured in upon him. The
case was quashed and he went free with no worse effects than an injury to his health.

As Civil War drew on Campbell hoped that the
issue might be submitted to arbitration, but he feared
that bloodshed was inescapable. When the war broke
out, the college was bereft of most of its students.
His own powers were weakening, but he kept busy.
In the absence of much teaching he took time to write
a biography of his father, Thomas Campbell. Gradually he loosed his hold upon life as a tree drops its
autumn leaves, and breathed his last a year after the
war was over, in 1866.

Sixty years have seen interdenominational conflict
steadily diminish, and in its place has come a trend towards Christian federation and unity. Before Campbell's death such undenominational Christian organizations as the Evangelical Alliance and the Young
Men's Christian Association had come into existence.
The broadening work of the Christian Association has
made men forget the unessentials in favour of the com-

mon base of Christian faith and experience, and has
created an organization for active service to individuals
and groups. Campbell was a pioneer of interdenomi-
nationalism at a time when it was judged as harshly
by denominationalists as is internationalism by thoroughgoing nationalists. But he blazed the trail; others
have smoothed and illuminated it.

15

WILLIAM ELLERY CHANNING

W HEN Campbell and his contemporaries were
debating religious issues on the public platform in the West, the New England Congregationalists were breaking apart over questions of
theological doctrine. The Congregationalism of New
England, like the Presbyterianism of the Middle
States, was Calvinistic in theology. Both had their
model in Geneva in Calvin's time. Both stressed the
all-mightiness of God and the helplessness of man.
Both made a man's salvation depend on the sovereign
decree of God. Such a doctrine, however well adapted
it may have been to a period of strenuous religious and
moral reform like the sixteenth century in Europe, in
time had a tendency to grow irksome in a country like
America, which was beginning to assert human rights.
On the frontier Methodism was declaring that man had
power to approach God and accept His way of salvation in Christ. In New England, where the first battles
of the Revolution were fought, insurgents against Calvinism began to direct their hot shot against the old
doctrines as early as the time of Jonathan Edwards.

Prominent pioneers in the effort to get a higher appreciation of human nature and its possibilities were
Charles Chauncy and Jonathan Mayhew. Chauncy
was pastor of the First Congregational Church in
Boston, Mayhew of the West Church. When Jonathan

Edwards published his *Narrative* of the Northampton revival, Chauncy put into print certain *Seasonable Thoughts* on the subject, which showed that he regarded such emotional revivalism as unhealthful. He desired a calmer, less spasmodic cultivation of religion by means of the services of worship and other aids supplied by the churches. Mayhew went farther. He opposed the belief in the Trinity altogether, republished the books of English Unitarians, and may be called the first of New England Unitarians.

These men pointed out the way in which the opposition to Calvinism was moving. Puritanism with its pessimistic opinion about the worth of man was on the wane. The tendency was to stress human values and the innate possibilities of religious development without those spiritual convulsions that orthodox revivalists believed were tokens of the working of the Holy Spirit upon such souls as were destined to be saved. As the liberals in their theology added dignity to man, they similarly subtracted something of man's belief in the sovereignty of God. They were especially skeptical about the essential place of Christ as an atoning Saviour, and they leaned towards the Arian opinion, then in vogue in the Church of England, that Christ was divine but not fully God.

The New England theology of Edwards and Hopkins had modified the unadulterated Calvinism of the Puritan fathers. But Edwardeanism was no more satisfactory to men like these. It was a question how long men with liberal ideas would remain in fellowship with clergy of the older kind, and quite a question whether

the bulk of the laity would put up with liberal preaching.   The laity is usually more conservative than the
clergy, having less time or inclination to think pro-
gressively in a field that is not well understood by those
who are untrained to theological thinking.   But both
parties were reluctant to see any division of forces.
Certain groups of Separatists had drawn off from the
Congregational churches after the Great Awakening.
It would be a pity if more divisions should take place
because some minds were restive under the old discipline.

Before any break came in the ranks of Congregationalism, a single Episcopal church in Boston became
Unitarian.   This was King's Chapel, the oldest Episcopal church in Massachusetts.   Eastern Massachusetts was the hotbed of liberal thinking, but it was
not all Congregational.   James Freeman, a young
preacher of liberal tendencies, who was familiar with
English Unitarianism, was the instrument through
whom the change was made.   In the absence of any
bishop liberal enough to ordain him he was ordained
by vestrymen of King's Chapel, where he had been a
lay reader.   He became pastor of the church, was outspoken in his advocacy of Unitarianism, and the
church became transformed in its denominational relations.   For fifty years after his ordination in 1784
Freeman was admired as a fearless exponent of religious liberalism, though not in entire harmony with
most New England Unitarians regarding the doctrine
of the nature of Christ.

Four years before Freeman's ordination a boy was

born at Newport, Rhode Island, who was to become
the knight in shining armour of New England Unitarianism. This was William Ellery Channing. He inherited high qualities of personality from both sides
of the family, was reared in an environment of culture, and received the best education that New England could give to such a lad. Serious in disposition
and studious in habits, he gained much from his college course at Harvard, which he completed with the
class of 1798.

One day he was reading English philosophy under
a clump of willows in Cambridge, from which he could
look away across the marshes to the distant hills, when
he saw as in a vision the dignity of human nature.
He was thrilled as he mused upon the possibilities of
humanity. As other men had a religious experience
of God, so he had an experience of man, in whose
nature he had a share, and he longed to give his vision
to others. He gave himself further to philosophical
study, and after a time he resolved that the Christian
ministry should be his life-work.

Like several of the prominent Puritan preachers
reared in England in the days of colonial settlement
Channing spent some years as a private tutor. This
occupation took him to Richmond, Virginia, for five
years. Those years broadened his education by
bringing him into contact with the South and its institutions. They helped to intensify his dislike for
slavery which he knew at first hand in his boyhood
Newport, the centre of the American slave trade. The
years there altered somewhat his political outlook.

They gave him dreams of social reform.   From a boy he grew into a man.   But his health suffered from too much mental application and seclusion, and he returned to the North with a weakened constitution.   He was dangerously introspective, inclined to take a gloomy view of life, and conservative in his theological opinions.

His return to Newport brought him under the pulpit influence of Samuel Hopkins, the eminent interpreter of the New England theology, and he remained evangelical in thought and preaching.   In 1803 he accepted a call to become minister of the Federal Street church, Boston, and there had an opportunity to express his opinions as they had matured in his mind.   The building in which the people worshipped was a plain, barn-like structure, built originally by the Presbyterians. It obtained some fame because of the meeting there of the state convention that favoured ratification of the federal constitution, and that event gave its name to the street.   The Boston of that day has been described as like an English market town, with a population of about twenty-five thousand persons.   Men still wore the picturesque costume familiar in the Revolution, and practised the social graces of colonial days. Massachusetts was Federalist in politics, and its delegates in Congress were prominent in that body.   Religion in Boston was mainly of the Congregational sort; ministers generally were liberal in theology, but they needed enlivening in their preaching.

Into this environment came Channing.   It was good for him to have a church to occupy his energies, but his thoughts continued to turn in upon himself more than was good for him. But his earnest devotion to the things of the spirit attracted to him people who were truly religious, and it became necessary to build a larger house of worship. He made his home in the parsonage in the rear of the meeting-house, and invited his mother and brothers and sisters to live with him. As he improved in health and cheerfulness under the influence of this home life, his theology broadened. He thought less of human depravity and more of divine love, less of the necessity of conversion and more of salvation as a process. Gradually the fatherhood of God became the central doctrine of his theology. Before long Unitarians were looking to him as their future leader. Even yet Congregational ministers were slow to announce themselves Unitarian, partly because they disliked the radicalism of contemporary English Unitarians.

Harvard College had been established in the first decade of the Massachusetts Bay settlement as a training-school for the future ministry in New England. It was sternly Congregational when its first president, Henry Dunster, became a Baptist, and the college would not keep him in office. It had shown signs of liberalism in the time of Increase Mather, and a half century later had opposed the evangelism of Whitefield. In 1805 it showed its unorthodox sympathies by electing Henry Ware, minister of the church at Hingham, as Hollis professor of divinity. Ware was not offensively pugnacious in his theology, but he was a well-known liberal, and it seemed that Harvard had committed itself to the Unitarian party in the Congregational church, then the established church in Massachusetts.

Other evidences of a drift towards Unitarianism were appearing. Congregational churches in Worcester and Portland divided, and the historic Plymouth church of the Mayflower Pilgrims became definitely Unitarian shortly before Channing went to Boston. Newspaper controversy began between liberals and conservatives. Park Street church was established in Boston to hold the fort for orthodoxy, and Andover Seminary to counteract the influence of Harvard. Unitarian was a stricter term than liberal. The two were by no means synonymous. A man might be unsound in a number of ways, but he was not a Unitarian unless he disbelieved in the doctrine of the Trinity. As yet Unitarians were unseparated from orthodox Congregationalism, and when the break came many liberals remained in the Congregational fold. By 1815 Unitarian ministers were avowing their beliefs frankly from the pulpits of Congregational churches, and one by one churches were declaring themselves until more than a hundred were lost to Trinitarian Congregationalism, including nearly all of the old and leading churches of eastern Massachusetts.

Channing was aroused to the defense of liberal principles by an attack upon American Unitarianism as a radical movement like English Unitarianism. He was then thirty-five years old, naturally averse to controversy, but ready for it if it must come. He wrote letters defining his own position, and contributed periodical articles that clarified the situation. But it was his historic sermon at Baltimore in 1819 that drew the line sharply between Trinitarians and Unitarians, and was followed shortly by division and reorganization among the churches.

The occasion of the sermon was the ordination of Jared Sparks, who later became president of Harvard College. The Unitarian church in Baltimore was with Charleston the bulwark of liberal opinion in the South. Channing was invited as a distinguished representative of New England Unitarianism. No better opportunity could be given for a challenge to Calvinists of the Congregational churches. Like Wesley in the Church of England, Channing had no desire to separate from the old church of New England, but he summoned the orthodox to the bar of reason and conscience. The sermon was published and enjoyed a surprising circulation. In those days everybody was interested in religion, and everybody wanted to know what the Unitarian movement signified.

The first distinctive feature of Unitarianism was its championship of the essential dignity of man as opposed to the Calvinistic doctrine of total depravity. The first consequence of such a belief was in the direction of greater human freedom, and it was logical that Channing should become the apostle of human freedom. He was enthusiastic over European revolutions that were taking place about 1820, giving promise of emancipation from tyranny. He became eloquent over the wrongs of the slave. He pleaded for freedom of religious thinking. He was a force for righteousness in his pulpit in Federal Street, in temperance, prison reform, education, international peace. It was an age when philanthropy and social reform were coming to the front, and his church and fellow Unitarians were deeply sympathetic with all of it. Small wonder is it that a denomination which needed just such leadership as Channing gave it in its formative period should idolize him. Channing's influence has not been confined to his own denomination. The possibilities that are latent in the human soul have revealed themselves more fully since Channing lived, and whatever one's creed may be one believes more readily in freedom and brotherhood and human worth because Channing lived.

A second positive principle of Unitarianism was the ability of man to work out his own salvation through the cultivation of the best that is in him, and not to depend on an atonement for sin wrought out by another person. It was at this point that Unitarians differed so sharply from orthodox evangelicals. Evangelicals might become lukewarm in their Calvinism, accepting rather the Arminian doctrine of free grace, but they trusted to a divine Saviour for salvation. In denying that Christ was full deity Unitarians removed the prop that Christians had had for their faith. The Channing Unitarians took a less radical position than have later Unitarians, believing that Christ is more than man and still a Saviour. Channing said: " A majority of our brethren believe that Jesus Christ is more than man; that He existed before the world; that He literally came from heaven to save our race;

that He sustains other offices than those of teacher and witness of the truth; and that He still acts for our benefit and is our intercessor with the Father." But the Unitarian struck a blow at the citadel of the Christian faith when he questioned the full dignity of the person of Christ.

A third cardinal belief of the Unitarians was the immanence of God. That doctrine of Greek Christianity had been overshadowed completely by Roman influence, and neither Protestant nor Puritan had recovered it. It was easier to believe that man could work out his own salvation when God was working within him to accomplish that purpose. And the doctrine of divine immanence supported the theory of the dignity of man. Ralph Waldo Emerson was the prophet of the immanence of God, and the liberalizer of Unitarian thought in his day.

Unitarians never have favoured creedal expression of religion and they have not agreed as to its content. Always certain men, like Theodore Parker, have been inclined towards radical opinions, but as steadily there have been more conservative men and women of more irenic temper. Unitarianism is best regarded as an attitude of mind rather than a theological system. It has stood for human worth and freedom as its principal constructive contribution. Organized in the American Unitarian Association in 1825, the Unitarian movement attracted liberals who found themselves out of place in the evangelical denomination. It appealed especially to thoughtful people of culture and liberal opinions rather than to those who needed a gospel for men of sin. It made a name for itself in literature and philanthropy. It has had a strong influence in liberalizing religion, and is properly estimated as a pioneering force for freedom of thinking far more powerful than its numbers would lead one to expect.

When Channing was thirty-four years of age he married his cousin and child playmate, Ruth Gibbs. His health was never robust, and he travelled some years later in northern New England and New York, getting more enjoyment than physical profit from his journey. The next year, in 1822, he set out for Europe on a year's leave of absence. He found stimulus in contacts with men like Wordsworth and Coleridge. He did not gain in health, and after his return he required an assistant in the work of his parish. But he took part in Unitarian activities. He contributed to the columns of the new denominational weekly, the *Christian Register*. The Berry Street Conference of ministers which he had organized in Boston proved to be a safety valve for the expression of a variety of liberal opinions. He was chosen president of the Association, but pleaded his physical debility.

As the slavery controversy intensified Channing was drawn into its discussions. He did not like the militant tone of the early Abolitionists, and in his attempt to clarify the issue between parties he was criticised by both. In time he was certain to ally himself with the anti-slavery group, and soon he was writing letters and pamphlets on the subject. He had to guard his health continually, and took long vacations at Newport. His frailty increased with the years. He was

happy in his family and in his garden, for he loved
nature and felt it akin to the spiritual. He was intellectually keen and fond of meditation, but he
reached the heights of his greatness in his moral convictions and in his loyalty to the spiritually good.

His address at Philadelphia in 1841 on the Present
Age added to his reputation as a champion of freedom
and universal sympathy. These were characteristic
notes of speech and pen. It was impracticable for
him to continue to preach in Boston, and he realized
that his years were numbered. In 1841 he collected
and published his works in five volumes, and a sixth
volume was added two years later. After he had
preached for the last time in his Federal Street church,
which was on the occasion of his sixty-second birthday,
he started on a journey that he had long anticipated to
the interior of Pennsylvania, but the season was in-
clement, and presently he was in the Berkshire Hills
of western Massachusetts. After an anti-slavery address to the people who seemed lukewarm on the subject, he went on into Vermont, where he died.

Channing's place as the great pioneer of his liberal
faith rests secure. Frail in body, he was great in
soul. Loving peace he was forced into controversy.
He was loyal to his convictions, though they ran counter
to traditional faith and seemed to the unorthodox unchristian. His monument stands in the Public Garden
in Boston a reminder to every passer-by of a brave
life, different from but no less honoured than that of
Phillips Brooks, whose memorial stands in Copley
Square but a few blocks away.

16

HORACE BUSHNELL

THE Unitarian reaction against Calvinism which swept so many Congregational churches of eastern Massachusetts away from their ecclesiastical moorings had no great effect upon the rest of New England. But a gentler tide was moving Connecticut Congregationalism. It was like the difference between a tidal wave and a mild surge that makes a vessel restless on a choppy sea. The calm conservatism that had lasted after the excitement of the Great Awakening kept the Edwardean theology intact until the nineteenth century. But then began the drift to a new theological position within the Congregational ranks.

The strongest influence in the new direction was at Yale College. First President Dwight, a grandson of Jonathan Edwards, and then Professor Nathaniel Taylor taught doctrines which came to distinguish the so-called " New Haven theology " from the New England theology, and caused so much alarm among thirty of the Congregational ministers that they organized a conservative union and then undertook to establish a new theological seminary, which later found its home in the capital of the state as the Hartford Theological Seminary. This was occurring soon after the Unitarian separation had taken place in Massachusetts.

One of the students who came under Taylor's instruction at Yale about 1830 was Horace Bushnell. He had been born at Litchfield, Connecticut, in 1802. He was of good New England stock. His father was a farmer, like most men of his day. He had been reared an Arminian rather than a Calvinist, and his wife was an Episcopalian. With these religious antecedents the boy was never indoctrinated in that rigid Calvinism which was the bane of many a New England boy. After the family removed to New Preston where Horace grew up, Congregationalism furnished the only opportunity for church connection, but the boy learned to discriminate between religion and the New England theology.

After the manner of the time he worked hard at manual labour intermingled with the cultivation of his mind. He went to school with other boys and used his books conscientiously, but much of his education came from nature. The rolling hills and flowing streams of Litchfield County made an environment in which he delighted; he loved nature, and became acquainted with nature's ways. Before he left home he joined the church with a deep sense of his religious obligation. He entered Yale College at the age of twenty-one, and there found it difficult to square his faith with his reason, and he was tormented by a tendency to doubt the accepted theology. After graduation he experimented with teaching, then with editorial work on the *New York Journal of Commerce,* and then went back to Yale to study law. This he continued for two years, coupled with tutoring in the college. As he was about ready for admittance to the bar he passed through a transforming religious experience which turned him to the ministry.

That experience of Bushnell changed his whole mental attitude. He had been beset by intellectual difficulties. Until those problems were solved there seemed to be no way of escape. But he was helped to see that religion is less of the head than of the heart, less of the intellect and more of the feelings and the will. A reading of Coleridge's *Aids to Reflection,* a book that revealed to Bushnell something of the new thought of England and the Continent, was his first reminder. The second came from his participation in a college revival, which brought to him a vivid sense of the validity of spiritual religion and the obligation to his pupils that he should take a positive position. Henceforth his outlook broadened and he became a shepherd, leading those who would follow him into new and greener pastures and beside streams of living water.

Once out of college leading strings Bushnell became minister to the North Congregational church, Hartford. He married, and made a home in a house built from his own plans and located where he could look off to a distance and could have a garden. Bushnell craved the long view of things, and he wanted a garden because of his love for nature. His people soon learned to love him and to admire his ability, and he was able to weld together diverse elements that were antagonistic over points of theology. Bushnell never had but the one pastorate, and he filled it full of rich ministry to others. When his books aroused criticism for their

unconventional way of putting things, his people stood
by him loyally.

He found a place in civic affairs, and did not forget
his responsibilities as a moulder of public opinion.
With commendable foresight he saw the possibilities
of the future Hartford, and through his personal influence the city set aside a part of the centre of the
community for a public park, which fitly bears his
name, and determined on a more suitable location of
the State capitol. It was Bushnell also who won for
the community an excellent system of public water
works.

Bushnell was by inclination a scholar. His sermons
were thoughtful rather than eloquent, and he spent
many hours in his study turning over in his mind the
theological problems that seemed to the church people
of those days so important a part of religion. Congregationalism, soundly Calvinistic though it was,
could not escape the influence of the new thinking that
was stirring in both Europe and America, and Bushnell
would not if he could. He was not intimately acquainted with the trend of thought in Germany, except as he got it at second hand from Coleridge. But
a revolution in thought had come there. Some time
earlier Kant, the philosopher, had criticised pure reason and had fallen back upon practical judgments of
experience as the only valid dependence of a man.
And now Schleiermacher was teaching, as Bushnell
had come to see, that the Christian religion is a matter
of the soul's inner experience rather than of endless
cogitation, that the feelings are to receive recognition

as an instrument of the divine spirit, and that faith
is an assurance of things unseen. With faith and feeling leading him along the way and reason correcting
his steps, he moved to a new theological position. It
was in sight of the Unitarian camp, but Bushnell refused to go so far.

His first distinct contribution to better thinking was
in the field of religious approach to God. The Old
Calvinists maintained that man in his total depravity
could do nothing but rely on means of grace, such as
attendance upon religious worship, and wait for God to
come to him. The Edwardeans believed and used revivalistic methods so that man could be put where
God could bring about his conversion. Bushnell
waved aside both doctrines, denied the essential sinfulness of human nature, and argued in a book on
Christian Nurture that God's grace might gently lead
the individual from early years to his Father's house,
so that a child rightly reared need never know the
necessity of conversion. In this gentle leading the
parents must be the guides. Thus Bushnell stressed
the solidarity of the family and the responsibility of
parents. At one stroke he abandoned the prevailing
evangelistic principles of his time, which was the *motif*
of missions abroad and revivalism at home, for a religious education which should make it easy to persuade a man that he was already a child of God.

Bushnell's reaction was a healthy one against a too
exclusive method of emotional disturbance, but his
critics thought that he underestimated the prevalence
of sin and its grip upon those whose habits are formed,

and the necessity of a radical change that would mean a right-about-face in conduct and purpose. Bushnell gives another evidence, like the Unitarian reaction, that a revolt from an extreme doctrine like Calvinism is likely to carry the thinker far towards the opposite extreme.

Bushnell had published his first book in 1846. Three years later he was ready with another, which was the result of a clearer vision that came to him of Christ as the indwelling force that makes for righteousness. By a spiritual illumination he gained a new assurance that religion was not to be proved logically, like a mathematical proposition, but learned by vivid inner experience of God. This gave him his theme for three addresses that year at the divinity schools of Harvard, Yale, and Andover, a text for more than one sermon, and the subject for discussion in his *God in Christ*. Bushnell tried to make it clear that the conception of the Trinity was a profound truth, but that God was a unity, working and revealing Himself in different aspects as Father, Son, and Spirit. He could be understood through experience, if not by reason.

Such opinions as these aroused quick protest. His opponents were after him with hue and cry. Prominent religious journals attacked him. The Hartford Central Association, of which he was a member, examined his book, but refused to condemn the author. By appeal the matter was brought before the General Association of Congregational churches in Connecticut and pressed on several occasions, but the decision was against disciplining Bushnell. His own North church in Hartford, loyal to its pastor, smarted under the charges of heresy that were laid on the minister and voted to withdraw from the Association, and in its proud independency to make its pastor free. So Bushnell won his triumph.

The attacks left their marks upon Horace Bushnell, and physically he bent under the storm. While his courage was unshaken and his convictions firm, the flesh quivered under the lash of criticism. He went away for a time to recover his poise, travelled first to North Carolina, then to Europe, and later through the new West, going as far as the Pacific coast, where he had a share in founding the University of California. Again in his pastorate he entered into the religious awakening of 1857, but by 1859 he found himself unable to continue in the regular pastorate, and his resignation was accepted by his reluctant people.

Meantime he had been engaged in the writing of another book, which was published in 1858 with the title, *Nature and the Supernatural*. He had tried to make plain the essential unity of God and the fact of God's redeeming love in Christ. Now he hoped to show that God and nature were likewise a greater unity than men had thought. God was not to be thought of as apart from His world, compelled to interfere miraculously and set things right, but moving along the avenues of cause and effect and ruling nature as Himself within it. Man is God's natural creation and so a part of the world of nature, but in his spirit he moves in the supernatural sphere, and is akin to

God in both. When other thinkers affirmed a great gulf fixed between God and the world, it was revolutionary to say such things as he said, but he was leading many minds afield to range more widely and to look on God unafraid. The tenth chapter of the book on the Character of Jesus was issued independently at a later date, and became a classic on the subject.

In spite of shattered health, for tuberculosis had fastened itself upon him, he wrote on, feeling that he had a further contribution to make towards the reconstruction of Christian thought. He was not a systematic theologian, but he felt the urge to express for others the experience that had come to himself. In 1866 he followed the expansion of his ideas on the meaning of Christ's atonement for sin. The title of the book was the *Vicarious Sacrifice*. The prevailing opinion about the atonement in evangelical circles was the governmental theory that Christ had been substituted for the sinner to bear the penalty of sin which was required to satisfy the justice of God, and thus was released the forgiving grace of God. This was a theory congenial to the speculative intellect of Congregational theologians, but not to the heart of Bushnell, and it was a theory that seemed to him untrue to the character of God as revealed by Jesus. Instead of thinking of Christ as mollifying the aggrieved heart of God, or suffering the penalty of His wrath or justice, Bushnell regarded Christ as the expression of the heart of a God who yearned for His prodigal children, seeking to reconcile them to Himself. He believed that the Cross by the power of its moral influence wins men to

God.   Love is always vicarious, and so the sacrifice of Christ was vicarious, but not substitutionary.   That was the thesis of the writer, and with love as his central principle he warmed human hearts that were chilled by their theology at the spiritual fire that glowed in his own soul.

Like a true Christian patriot Horace Bushnell was interested in all good causes.   He preached on national questions, including slavery, when they were uppermost in the public mind.   He opposed the growth of Catholicism in the United States, when it was gathering strength through immigration.   He made numerous college addresses.   At one time he was asked to accept the presidency of Middlebury.   Both Wesleyan and Harvard granted him the degree of doctor of divinity, and Yale honoured him with the doctorate of laws.   In later life, after he was freed from pastoral responsibilities he delivered many addresses before colleges, seminaries, and religious conventions. In some of these addresses, as in a discussion of the growth of law at New Haven, he laid down principles that since then have become recognized as fundamentally sound, but then were contrary to current theory.

His essays were the fruit of hard thinking.   He liked to face hard problems, as when he grappled with the problem of the moral values of hard experiences. In his *Work and Play* he makes plain that work for a definite end may become a joy, and that this is what life is intended to do for a man.   An essay on religious music was a reminder to his friends, not only that he was fond of melody and familiar with music, but also that he had founded the Beethoven Society when a student at Yale.

Bushnell was happy in his home life. He had a wife who was sympathetic with his ideals, and happy in the making of his home. He liked to frolic with his children, and recognized a time for play as well as for work. Out-of-door activity especially appealed to him. He was in the habit of getting up early to dig in his garden or swing his scythe. Then when the family had assembled, he was fresh from the bath, ready for breakfast and the day's task. At the breakfast table he discussed the news of the world which the morning paper brought, illuminating it with his stock of knowledge on all sorts of subjects. In normal health he was a man of vigour and energy, ready to crack hard nuts intellectually, and welcoming a challenge to physical effort. After he passed into the sixties with broken health, he could not measure up to his former standards, but he kept manfully at his desk to the last. His character mellowed as he aged, and his mystic sense of God deepened especially under the influence of nature, which to him always spoke of God. This, which was always a meaningful thought to him, runs through his last book, *Forgiveness and Law*. In this study he was on the border of the great discovery of the evolutionary process, but he passed it by unseeing. It was not lack of appreciation but of scientific investigation, and if Bushnell could not be both saint and scientist, one would rather take him for what he was.

Up to the approach of the end of his life his thoughts

were active. He planned a volume on the methods
and values of inspiration, but he wrote only a few
chapters. In the spring of 1875 he was very ill, but
recovered slowly. Strolling in the park, he enjoyed
the erection of the State capitol on the spot which he
had selected. The illness returned a year later and
he sank peacefully to rest on the seventeenth of Febru-
ary, 1876.

Horace Bushnell was a pioneer of liberal evangelical
thought. He tried to make religion more natural and
more easily understood, and he succeeded in making it
easier for minds essentially evangelical to find their way
through to the best thought of a later time. He did
much to give warmth to theology as well as new light
to the Church. He will always hold a large place in the
history of Christian thought because he humanized
God, as Jesus did, and turned the currents of New
England thinking into fresh and fruitful channels. He
was not a Unitarian. The divine Christ was too vividly
real to him to make that possible. But he knew that
if Jesus Christ was to be a real Saviour and Friend to
men, He must be thought of not as an alien from another sphere but naturalized into full citizenship in the
earth, if not a native of its soil. He was a man who
never rested content with the visions of truth that he
had gained, and he inspired other men to take up the
themes that he had studied and to carry them farther.

He died too soon to become indoctrinated in the
scientific thought of the last quarter of the nineteenth
century. He belonged to the period of escape from the
blight of the old theology of New England, but in his

flight from prison he did not fall into any quagmire of
uncertainty. He had a positive gospel and he craved
it for the youngest of God's children. He was a path-
breaker in the new field of religious education. He
was no specialist in the method, but he had a strong
grasp of the principle that in every one is the capacity
to know and love God, and that the germ of the divine
can unfold under the sunshine of love into noble, beautiful personality. Such he was in his own example as
well as teaching.

17

DWIGHT LYMAN MOODY

THE Connecticut River is a small stream among historic rivers, but on its banks lived three of the men whose stories are included in this book. From Bushnell's Hartford it is forty miles upstream to Northampton, where Jonathan Edwards aroused the consciences of his hearers with his fiery discourse. Thirty miles farther north at Northfield was the home of the best known of nineteenth century evangelists in the English speaking world, Dwight Lyman Moody.

Moody was of Puritan ancestry, connected with families that had lived for two hundred years on the farms of the fertile intervale of the Connecticut. More than one of his relatives made bricks for the houses of his neighbours. Dwight was born in 1837, the year in which Queen Victoria ascended the throne of Great Britain, the year of grave financial difficulties in the American world of finance, following the radical fiscal policy of the President, Andrew Jackson. While still a boy his father died suddenly, and the widow with a large family of small children was burdened heavily by poverty. Dwight grew up disciplined in its school, early in life learning to be industrious, and disciplined by a conscientious mother in the home until he learned the essentials of good character. He was a real boy,

196

sharing in pranks with other boys and usually their leader.

After various experiments at earning money, sandwiched in between his schooling, the boy left his valley home for Boston when he was about seventeen years old, and found employment in the store of an uncle. His native gifts soon made him a successful salesman, and he tried the new method of soliciting trade on the street. Thus early he showed characteristics that were to serve him later in his life-work of evangelism.

Dwight's uncle had exacted from his nephew a promise that he would attend church regularly, if he took him into his business. He went to a Congregational church on Beacon Hill near the gilt-domed State capitol and joined a Bible class for young men. It was there that he began to get acquainted with the Bible. Moody's mother had trained her large family of children in the essentials of religion, but the boy acquired no familiarity with the Bible. This deficiency was made up during the years in Boston. Under the tactful guidance of his teacher he was brought to make a personal commitment of himself to Christ, and after the church was satisfied that his conversion was genuine it admitted him to its membership.

After two years in Boston with its conservative business methods, Moody was attracted to the bustling city of Chicago in 1856. He soon found employment, and from the beginning allied himself with the church. Already his energy was seeking an outlet in some form of Christian service, and he hit upon the method of hiring a pew in the church and inducing young men wherever he found them to occupy the pew with him on Sunday. The one pew presently became four, and almost before he realized it the young business man found himself in the midst of the revival of religion that swept the country in 1857.

His success as a boot and shoe salesman commended him to his employer, and he was sent out as a commercial traveller to represent the business house. He enjoyed the stir of life in the Middle West, and had an ambition to make money rapidly, like most young men who went West. He was popular with other men, and soon interested himself in their spiritual welfare. Born of Congregationalist parents who believed in sin and definite conversion, he was interested to save sinners to a better life and purpose.

Moody was a successful business man. By the time he was twenty-four he was making five thousand dollars a year and had saved considerable money. He had cherished large ambitions, but these fell away as he became more and more absorbed in his religious activities. He reached the point where he was ready to give all his time to Christian work, and he sacrificed all regular income, planning to live as long as he could on his savings. He was interested in children, and he gathered them into North Market Hall, riding around town with them on a pony that he purchased to aid him in his undertaking. He used novel methods to catch and hold boys, and some of them became so attached to him that they were known popularly as Moody's bodyguard.

Such conduct aroused public attention, and he was

sometimes spoken of contemptuously as "Crazy Moody." Nothing of that sort disturbed him. He hunted out country boys who were running wild in the city. He held evangelistic meetings on his own account, sometimes speaking himself, oftener getting other men to make the addresses. He became active in the Chicago Young Men's Christian Association, where he was leader of a number of young men in personal Christian work. He was developing the powers and acquiring the characteristics that were to make him famous in later days.

When the Civil War broke out he threw himself into meetings for the soldiers passing through the city and in camps near by. These meetings were connected with the Young Men's Christian Association, and later the work was affiliated with the Christian Commission. Subsequently the camp was turned into a detention camp for Southern prisoners, and Moody evangelized among them with encouraging results. After some of the more important battles of the war he was on the ground aiding the wounded and in the hospitals where he did the work of a chaplain. Moody was ready to step into the breach whenever an opportunity offered for kindly service or public address. When nothing special drew him away, he was busy in the noon prayer-meetings of the Young Men's Christian Association in Chicago.

After the war was over he decided that Sunday School work should be his chief employment, and Illinois was soon organizing itself for better schools. Moody was among its officers and most active sup-

porters.   But he was experimenting with revivalistic
meetings, and was beginning to receive invitations to
hold meetings out in the country.   Sometimes he
turned a Sunday School convention into an evangelistic
meeting.   A new church grew out of his North Market
Hall Sunday School in 1863, and Moody became a deacon of the church.   At a large convention Moody and
Sankey met for the first time, and after some months
the two men linked their fortunes for the enterprise of
evangelism.   Sankey's singing was the complement to
Moody's preaching from that time.

Visitors from England sometimes came to Moody's
acquaintance, and his deep interest in both the Sunday
School and the Young Men's Christian Association
made him wish to profit from English experiences.
In his characteristic fashion he made a sudden decision
to go to England for observation of methods.   There
he found channels of expression, established relations
with Christian leaders, and started a noon prayer-
meeting in the London Young Men's Christian Association.   Similar meetings were held in other parts of
the city.   He was still feeling his way to the great task
of his life.   New experiences in America, including
the burning of Chicago, the erection of his first tabernacle in that city, another visit to England in which
his evangelistic preaching resulted in remarkable success, and he was fairly launched upon his career.

Revival meetings were not new in the early seventies.
From the time of Edwards and Whitefield and Wesley
they had continued intermittently, and successive
waves of evangelism had swept over America.   Such

methods were not acceptable to conservative bodies like the Church of England, but the English Dissenters made religion personal and called for active commitment of the soul to God. But Dwight Lyman Moody made use of new methods in his evangelism. Though unordained, he preached in pungent, homely fashion. Little educated, but increasingly familiar with the Bible, he expounded it in businesslike fashion, and directly urged people to accept the obligations of personal discipleship to Christ. After his preaching he adjourned the meeting to a smaller group of inquirers with whom he came to close quarters with personal appeals. Certain meetings he devoted to Bible readings, associating scattered selections to enforce the particular lesson that he wished to emphasize. People were encouraged to bring their Bibles with them, and this sort of attention to Scripture gave an impetus to further Bible study.

All-day meetings were tried on his first extended evangelistic tour in Great Britain. Beginning at eleven o'clock in the morning, an hour was spent in confession and prayer, and then another hour in praise. A promise meeting followed and then a witness meeting, both of which elicited the testimonies of Christians. The last two of the six-hour series included a Bible reading by Moody, and a communion service in which he was assisted by ministers. His lack of ordination discredited him with Episcopalians, but it did not disqualify him among the Dissenters.

Powerful as Moody was in his ability to move his hearers, he was assisted greatly by the musical fea-

tures of the meetings.   Sankey's singing which he accompanied on a cabinet organ, gave added zest to the
services and moved the hearts of the audience.   He
used certain gospel hymns that were then in customary
use in evangelistic services, and he drew upon others
of his own composition which he rendered with great
effect upon the crowds.   Few who heard him could
forget the melody or the words of such a simple song
as that of the lost sheep:

> " There were ninety and nine that safely lay
>   In the shelter of the fold,
>   While one was out on the hills away
>   Far off from the gates of gold."

For greater convenience a small collection was made
and printed of the songs used in the English meetings,
and then in America a larger collection was brought together under the title of *Gospel Hymns*.   The immense
popularity of this song book made it feasible to publish others until six books were on the market.   The
sales were enormous, but with characteristic generosity
the evangelists turned over the proceeds to religious
beneficence.   The completion of the Moody church in
Chicago rebuilt after the fire was thus made possible,
and other sums went to the construction of buildings
for the Northfield schools that Moody started.

The evangelistic success in the north of England in
1873 brought an invitation to go farther north into
Scotland.   At Edinburgh the largest hall in the city
was packed at one service after another.   There was
no great emotion in either the preaching or the reaction

to it, but an earnestness that could be felt as the
speaker pleaded with the people to yield their wills
to God. Scores of persons responded at every meeting until the number of converts mounted into the
hundreds. Others who had been interested earlier in
life but had lost their first thrill were won back to a
new religious vitality. Meetings were held for special
groups like workingmen. The crowds were so great
at the height of the campaign that tickets of admission
were distributed to make certain that the persons
wanted might get in. After weeks of such experiences
in Edinburgh the evangelists moved to other cities.
From Scotland they went to Ireland, and then to the
provincial cities of England where many thousands
hung on Moody's words.

After two years he yielded to the urging of many
that he would go to London. Formerly he did not feel
that there was unanimity enough among the ministers
to warrant the effort in the capital. But the newspapers had chronicled the progress of the campaigns,
and crowds were eager to see and hear when the meetings in London began. The streets near the place of
meeting were full of mocking men and women, but
great throngs of serious folk gathered day after day,
their spirits held in thrall by the Spirit of God. Anglicans as well as Baptists and Methodists sympathized,
and even the archbishop of Canterbury gave the meetings his unofficial endorsement. Charles H. Spurgeon,
the popular Baptist preacher at the Metropolitan
Tabernacle, assisted the evangelists heartily. The
weeks were filled with the usual general meetings, with

special services of various kinds, conferences, and conventions. Nearly six hundred ministers were present at the farewell meeting in London.

Known only to a limited circle of friends and fellow workers when he had sailed for Europe, Moody returned to America a conspicuous figure on account of his spectacular career abroad. At once he was besieged with invitations to visit the leading cities and conduct similar revivalistic campaigns. The largest cities provided him with enormous buildings for the meetings. In Philadelphia he had the use of the old Pennsylvania Railroad freight house, in Brooklyn of a rink, in New York of the famous Hippodrome. Chicago welcomed him back. Conservative Boston built him a tabernacle to seat six thousand persons, and for two months it was filled to overflowing several times a day. A moral awakening, especially in temperance, attended the religious movement.

Moody's meetings were remarkable for their success in the midst of a period of material prosperity in America, when interest in religion is usually at low ebb, and in the midst of a time of intellectual skepticism in England, when plain gospel preaching could hardly be expected to make much impression. But the evangelist went on his way unruffled, and the results justified his optimism. His preaching has been credited with helping effectually to stem the tide of doubt that had been sweeping over Great Britain.

The methods and results of the earlier campaigns were repeated in subsequent visits to England and tours in America. In the early 80's Moody was back in England and Scotland, and again in 1891–2. In the years between he was in active service in America. In his later years he appealed especially to lukewarm church people that he might enrich their experience.

One day as Moody was on a visit to his old home at Northfield he was stirred to the needs of the young people of the region for an education. The incipient institutions at Mount Holyoke and Wellesley stimulated his interest. In 1878 land was purchased for a seminary for young women and within a year classes were meeting and a recitation hall was rising. Other buildings followed, and Northfield Seminary with its intellectual opportunities and its religious atmosphere attracted students from far and near. The founder was not content with a girls' school. Boys, too, must be provided for. The establishment of Mount Hermon School followed. The first property was purchased in the year that the Seminary opened, and the School opened in 1881. It provided a special opportunity for boys with small pecuniary resources, by making it possible to aid themselves by working on the farm of two hundred and seventy-five acres. It was not long before these twin schools were making a deep impression on the life of hundreds of young people from far as well as near.

Out of Bible institutes for personal workers in the Chicago campaign of 1887 developed the Moody Bible Institute of that city. The plant was located near Moody's Chicago Avenue church. The Institute was opened in the fall of 1889, and men and women began to go out to evangelistic service, home and foreign missions, church work, and philanthropy, in ever-increasing numbers.

The increasing value of all these enterprises persuaded Moody to plan summer conferences at Northfield. These were inaugurated in 1880, and more than three hundred persons gathered, occupying the school buildings, filling the homes, and camping out in tents when no other quarters were available. Moody himself presided, but invited speakers from outside. The meetings were of a devotional character at first, but broadened to discuss the methods of Christian work, and to the various enterprises in which the Church is engaged. The conferences became more popular as the years passed. The best speakers were secured from England as well as America. Series of conferences were held during the summer, including gatherings of college students from colleges where the evangelist had spoken in previous years.

The various enterprises in which Moody was engaged filled his time full, but in 1892 he went to Palestine with members of his family and friends. He greatly enjoyed the visit, and preached to hundreds of people on the Mount of Olives. In 1893 he was carrying on an evangelistic campaign at the World's Fair at Chicago. In 1899 he yielded to an invitation to visit Kansas City for a preaching mission, and the results justified the undertaking. But he had used up vitality that needed replenishing. He returned to his Northfield home and at Christmas time his useful life came to an end. He was buried on Round Top, where so many hundreds of conference people had met again and again in prayer, and memorial services were attended by grieving multitudes all over the United States and Great Britain.

His single-hearted devotion to his religious task, his disinterestedness in all selfish concerns, his courage and faith in the midst of difficulties, and his remarkable successes in spite of his limitations of education, are among the characteristics that have given him prominence in the church history of the nineteenth century. His appreciation of education and his attention to it as an important part of his responsibility reveal the breadth of his mind. By the side of George Whitefield but moving on a larger stage will stand Dwight Lyman Moody in the annals of modern evangelism.

18

HENRY DRUMMOND

AMONG the assistants of Moody and Sankey on their first campaign in Scotland was a young man in the University of Edinburgh named Henry Drummond. Experience proved that he was fitted admirably to work evangelistically with young men, and he became Moody's main dependence for that side of his enterprise. The two men were unlike. The American was energetic and mature but uneducated, the Scotchman refined, young, well-trained. But they were complements of each other, and they became close friends and helpers.

Henry Drummond sprang from good native stock, and his home was in the historic country of Stirling, where he was born in 1851. He could look across to Stirling Castle and dream of the sovereigns who sojourned there, and he could look around on the plain of Bannockburn and imagine the scenes of the battle where Wallace with the Scots did bleed for Scottish independence from England. To the east was the capital Edinburgh, westward was the highland country of hills and lakes. The boy loved nature and delighted to roam amid its delights, to play where the burns tumbled down the hills and to fish for trout that lurked in the shady pools. After wide travels he came back to Stirling, and thought it without an equal anywhere.

At the age of fifteen he entered the University of

Edinburgh. He was slight in figure, and a bit afraid that he would not get a normal growth. He had a liking for natural science but did not take kindly to the classics. This early bent was an indication of his later career, but he could not know that then. He was seriously minded and conscientious, interested deeply in personal religion, and while he had no remarkable experience of conversion he drifted naturally to the place where the profession of the ministry made its appeal for his life's energies. Without getting his degree from the University, he enrolled in the divinity course of the Free Church at New College, Edinburgh. At that time certain college studies were included in the curriculum of Free Church theological schools, and Drummond kept his interest in his scientific studies.

In addition to his intellectual discipline he undertook an active part in carrying on a mission of one of the Free churches in the city, just in time to prepare him for the movement into which he was swept presently on the arrival of the American revivalists in Edinburgh. Drummond was attracted to the revival, particularly by the sincerity of Moody, and with a belief that these efforts for human salvation were needed, for he was a thorough Presbyterian. After some preliminaries he assumed the responsibility of certain meetings, and it was plain that he had found his place. Crowds flocked to the meetings that he conducted. Inquiring men opened their hearts to him and asked his advice. For the better part of two years he was immersed in this sweeping movement of evangelism, a man of wonderful power and success before

he was twenty-three years old. With all his fame he
was not spoiled, but remained the same attractive,
transparent nature, trusted and loved by those who
knew him.

When his work was done he resumed his interrupted
studies, unassuming and teachable. Humanly interested in the life of the school, he joined in its fun
as well as in its more sober affairs. He wore an air
of distinction, but not of pride, was eminently likable,
and his happy disposition enlivened those around him.
Meantime his mind broadened as he shared in the
newer methods of biblical study, which he linked with
his spiritual concerns and his evangelism. Once he
was through his theological course he considered his
future, spending his time in recreation and evangelism
during the summer. He declined several invitations to
ministerial settlement, not feeling sure as to what was
best. It was more than a year before he found his
place.

The Free Church College in Glasgow had a lectureship in natural science. The death of the lecturer left
a vacancy, and in 1877 Drummond was appointed to
the position. He gave instruction four times a week
to first year students in the elements of botany and
geology and in scientific method. In that formative
period of his career he was helped greatly by the
friendship of Marcus Dods, his pastor and associate
in a north of Glasgow mission for workingmen. For
four years he shared in the responsibilities of the mission until it became a full-fledged church. By the
time he gave way to an ordained minister Moody was

back in England on another tour of evangelism, and
Drummond found a place in the ranks of his helpers.
The closer acquaintance increased the regard of each
for the other.

It was at this time that Drummond mapped out his
book on *Natural Law in the Spiritual World*. His
studies of nature and his vivid experiences with the
inner spirit of man made him feel that there was such
close resemblance in their functioning that the same
laws must work in both. In both nature and the soul
was revealed the same unfolding of life and beauty
according to one law of evolution. That life could
come only from life was a principle that seemed to
apply to both nature and spirit, and without growth
comes degeneration. It all seemed simple, easy to
prove by the argument of analogy. Darwin had made
plain the scientific principle of evolution. There was
no question about the scientific method in nature.
Why is not the same method true in religion? Drummond had been coming to see that the spiritual nature
needed interpretation in modern terms, and he was
captivated by the possibilities of the principle of life
development when he came to apply it to the spiritual
nature of man.

Drummond's book met with a response that was
astonishing, except as one remembers that there was
a very widespread interest in the relation of science
and religion, and a book that seemed to bring the two
into such close harmony was very satisfying to those
who had been anxious about the conflict between the
two. The sale of the book was brisk, and the reputa-

tion that came to him was great. Yet, as the author saw later on, he had erred in his arguments, for he had failed to take sufficient account of the difference between the forces in each field of experience and of the necessity of moral effort to accomplish spiritual growth. Enamoured of the resemblances, he overlooked certain elements that had to be reckoned with. For that reason he came to regret his methods of discussion, but the fact remains that the book broadened the vision of many religious people, and helped them to see that science was not so mischievous as they had feared.

Between 1879 and 1891 Henry Drummond travelled far afield. The first journey was a geological expedition to the Rocky Mountains, which was enjoyable for the adventure in what was then a wild country, for the scientific interest, and for the close association with Geikie, the chief of the expedition. Geikie testified to the winsomeness of his companion, his enthusiasm in the day's work, and his pleasure in the scenery and in the human contacts. His next expedition was to central Africa, where for the first time he came to appreciate the importance of the foreign missionary enterprise. He was impressed profoundly with the degradation of the people and oppressed by the disease and slavery that they suffered. He realized how much precious life had been poured out in Africa by devoted missionaries. The contrast sobered him and gave him a new understanding. His discoveries in science were embodied in a volume on Africa. Later he made a third journey to the New Hebrides, which intensified his admiration for those who were·helping to hasten the development of uncivilized men into sons of God.

Between times the professor of science, who had been promoted from a lectureship to a chair of science, lectured to his pupils at Glasgow, who numbered about a hundred. He gave them schematic instruction in the specific sciences, but he helped them most by introducing them to nature as a department of divine handiwork that was not contrary to religion, and he showed them the age-long process by which the Divine Artificer had done His creative work. Probably the richest contribution that Drummond made to his time was his reconciliation of two fields of interest that seemed to be hostile to each other. In the process Drummond's own religion broadened—too much so, as it seemed to some—but he never lost his spiritual devotion, and he never sacrificed essential religion on the altar of science.

In one respect particularly did Drummond illuminate religion with the flashlight of science. That was in his interpretation of the Old Testament. He saw in the history of the Hebrew people as real a progress in religious understanding as the biological progress which he was familiar with in the evolution of animal life. God was creating the soul of a race in Egypt and Sinai and Canaan, revealing Himself by degrees as men could receive and appropriate the revelation, finding in the prophets His interpreters and in His Son the matchless expression of divinity. To Drummond this unfolding process was a piece with the slow creation of the natural world. Surely it was the same God who

works all in all.   That was the sublime teaching of his
time and to that he gave himself unstintedly.

Drummond loved young men and he wanted to show
them God and win them not only to understand but to
love him.   As he had opportunity he talked with them,
and on occasion he gathered them into public meetings and addressed them.   He knew instinctively the
life of youth by daily contacts and through many persons with whom he conversed about religion.   In the
eighties began a series of meetings with university students in Edinburgh and other student centres.   The
success of these religious meetings was so gratifying
that they resulted in visits by Drummond to university
centres in America as well.   Edinburgh remained for
years the centre of this student movement, as it was
the place of Drummond's professional task, but his influence extended from the classic halls of Oxford to
the fresh water colleges of interior America.

In the summer of 1887 Moody invited Drummond to
participate in a student conference at Northfield.   This
was the beginning of an acquaintance with Northfield
audiences which were inclined to be critical of Drummond's modernism but could not question his spirituality.   The visitor was well known in America from
his books, and he was the recipient of numerous invitations to lecture.   Summer assemblies of eager-minded
persons were coming into vogue.   The Chautauqua
movement had been started.   Drummond was interested in this attempt to popularize education, and
he was a welcome speaker on the Chautauqua platform.   He might have lectured on scientific themes at

many colleges. But his deepest concern was with the
spiritual life of college men, and he gave himself most
fully to the task of building character. He was able
to naturalize religion in the colleges, to make it seem
less remote from actuality, to give it expression in
service. Something about his youth, his direct
methods of approach, and his evident sincerity coupled
with recognized ability, gave him persuasive power
with college men.

Australian students were frequently in attendance
at the University of Edinburgh, and in 1889 Drummond was invited to go out to Melbourne University,
and other colleges showered him with invitations when
it was found that he might go. This journey gave him
the opportunity to visit the New Hebrides, and particularly to stop in Japan. In that far-away corner of
the world he found men with the same needs and
difficulties, eager to enlist his sympathy and to profit
from his religious experience. To all such he lent a
willing ear and gave help and encouragement to the
utmost of his ability.

Drummond returned from his far journey to live his
bachelor life in his large house on the hill crest over-
looking the city of Glasgow. In it he had accumulated
relics of travel east and west, and an ample library.
From the house he looked out on the broad expanse
of country with its background of distant hills, and
northward he could see in imagination the fair lakes
of the highlands. He loved his country, and he
thought and wrote better when he could see it in broad
perspective.

His return brought to him many criticisms of certain of his opinions expressed in print and in addresses, particularly a recent address at the College on the Christian Evolution of the World. He had many callers, usually in the evening. He gave his forenoons and free evenings to his books and writings; in the afternoon he walked or attended to his personal affairs. A wide correspondence kept him busy, for he did not employ a secretary. He was hospitable, and enjoyed having a friend as his guest for weeks at a time, but he seldom engaged in social recreation, except with students.

In 1893 he sailed for America to fill an engagement that he had made to give a series of Lowell Institute lectures in Boston. The Lowell Lectures are open to the public without charge, and a popular speaker draws large audiences. Drummond was known favourably to the Christian people of America, and he was speaking on the popular theme of evolution. Consequently the people thronged to hear him, and it was necessary to repeat the lectures twice in order to make it possible to satisfy the demand. The lecturer had been hard at work on his manuscript for weeks before he had left home, and after his return he prepared it for the press under the title of *The Ascent of Man*.

While he was in America he was in demand to speak at Harvard and Amherst colleges and at the World's Columbian Exposition at Chicago. Afterward he went to Chautauqua, where he repeated his Boston lectures, and then he visited Moody at the annual conference at Northfield. This time he was not happy in his visit, for his lectures brought upon him much criticism, and an attempt was made to prevent his speaking. Moody's confidence in his friend supported him. From Northfield he went on a vacation jaunt into Canada, where he had a few weeks at his favourite sport of fishing, and was then a guest of the Governor-General at Quebec. After a visit to the new University of Chicago, where he made addresses, he returned home by way of New York.

At the age of forty he was one of the leading figures of the religious world, experienced and travelled, and well known for his books and addresses. He might reasonably look forward to many years of ripe scholarship in his own chosen field and of useful service in church and college and Boys' Brigade. The last was especially on his heart. He plunged into his college tasks on his return, worked on the revision of his manuscript for the press, resumed his meetings for college students, and lectured here and there. But his health began to break. His American visit proved a strain upon his slender body, and the following winter made heavy demands upon him, and spring brought the beginning of a disease that fastened upon his life. He kept at his work as long as possible, and retained the cheerful, uncomplaining spirit that was characteristic of him. He maintained his interest in those matters of which he had been a part, and kept up communication with his friends by telegraph when he could no longer write. All efforts to relieve him were in vain, and in 1897 he went home. He was mourned wherever he had gone, from Glasgow to Australia and throughout

America, for a sweet and gallant spirit had departed from among men.

Henry Drummond lived at a time in Christian history when thoughtful persons were trying to adjust their Christian thinking to the new scientific knowledge which the nineteenth century was bringing in such abundance. That century was the century of natural science, as the twentieth century is the century of social science. Many discoveries in geology and biology brought a shock to people who were wonted to conventional doctrines and biblical interpretations, and they needed readjustment. Henry Drummond was an interpreter of the new with a firm grip upon the realities that were represented by the old. His value to his times lay in this. His evangelistic addresses showed his genuine religious spirit. His lectures revealed his knowledge of the scientific world. His *Ascent of Man* made it plain that a man could be a true Christian and at the same time welcome the new learning. For many persons evolution was christianized by Drummond. That he overemphasized in his books the point of his argument has been charged against him. He never could quite forget that in scientific writing he should not be an advocate. But for the public that took him for its guide it was the emphasis that recommended his writings. Certainly Drummond was a Christlike man in his disposition, in his devotion to the best, in his loyalty to noble ideals, in his faith and courage to the bitter end. The world was better because he had been in it. Religion was richer because he had interpreted it.

19

PHILLIPS BROOKS

WHEN Henry Drummond came to Boston to deliver his Lowell lectures in 1893 the city's greatest citizen had just ended his career. The man was Phillips Brooks, at one time the beloved rector of Trinity Church and subsequently the bishop of the diocese of Massachusetts. Both Brooks and Drummond were singularly lovable men, but Brooks came closer to people of every class in the pastoral relation and was almost worshipped by those who had been helped over hard places and through the depths of human experience. Brooks was the older man by sixteen years, but Drummond was in sight of the end when Brooks was taken. Both died in the full maturity of their powers before they were sixty years old.

Phillips Brooks was of Puritan ancestry, and he was minister of a church at the heart of the old Puritan colony of Massachusetts. Yet he reverted to the church of his English ancestors. Descended on his father's side from Reverend John Cotton of the original settlers and on his mother's side from the illustrious family of Phillips, benefactors of the academy and seminary at Andover, with such a man as Wendell Phillips for an uncle, he could not stifle his convictions though they might be contrary to hereditary teaching. His episcopalianism was not due to any whim of his own, but had the example of his mother who reacted

219

from the Unitarianism of Boston by going over to the Episcopal church.

Andover was the ancestral home, but the parents of Phillips Brooks made their home in Boston, and there he was born in 1835. Like Channing he had advantages of birth and breeding and a college education at Harvard. He entered into the college spirit, and there he caught the messages of Agassiz and Longfellow and Lowell, while outside college walls Emerson and Tennyson interpreted to him the larger life that was stirring at the middle of the nineteenth century. After an unhappy experience as a teacher in the Boston Latin School he went to the Episcopal Seminary at Alexandria, Virginia, to prepare himself for the clerical profession. He did not undertake the work of the ministry without deliberation. In college he was not very religious and with the critical attitude which college studies encourage he was not very responsive to the preaching that he heard from his Boston rector on Sundays. He does not seem to have been troubled seriously by intellectual difficulties, but he was slow to learn that nobility of life meant the commitment of will to the highest principles of service. Without any revolutionary experience but with a growing conviction that he was called to be a minister to his fellows in spiritual things, he took the advice of his pastor and went to Virginia before he was received into full membership in the church.

There can be no surprise to any one who knew the religious influences of his home life that Phillips Brooks should become a minister. His mother was a devout woman in whose heart burned a holy love for her Saviour, and that love was reflected in her life and in the training of her family. Her boys knew the secret of her devotion and the flame of her faith and love was kindled in their hearts at an early age. It was that magnet which drew the thoughtful boy into his sacred calling when his mind was in doubt over his course.

For a time he did not find himself in the Seminary, but by the second year he matured rapidly, achieved a reputation as a brilliant student, and at last found spiritual peace in a surrender of all that nineteenth century life so fully offered him to the will and service of God. In his conversion Phillips Brooks was a true representative of the age in which he lived. The decision that confronted him was not, as a century before, a choice between yielding to the cravings of life on its lower levels such as frontier urgings encouraged, and the cold far heights where dwelt the souls of the elect. Life presented a different aspect to the cultured mind of Phillips Brooks. He knew how ample it might be when enriched with the products of scientific study and literary lore. He was impressed with brilliant fancies of poets, the learned conclusions of scientists, and the brave attempts of philosophers to account for the problems of nature and human experience. Could he find such wealth of truth and experience in religion? Was the holy temple in which God dwelt the church or the world? This was his problem, but he found its solution in an honest willingness to learn the truth by doing the will of God.

Brooks found his first parish in Philadelphia at the

Church of the Advent, and later was transferred to Trinity church. He preferred to commence his ministry elsewhere than in Boston. In Philadelphia he found trial of his patience when the Civil War broke out. As at the time of the Revolution, the temper of the city was conservative, ready to compromise with slavery if not to submit to it, and fearful of mixing up the church with social issues. Brooks was outspoken in his unrelenting opposition to the whole system, arguing political questions and demanding loyalty to Christian principles. He soon won a reputation as a man of courage and as a good preacher.

The youthful minister took his profession seriously, but he did not neglect his playtime. He welcomed his vacations like a schoolboy, glad of an excuse to run home for a visit, up to Andover to his kinsfolk, or to Niagara or the White Mountains for relaxation and sightseeing. Before 1862 was over the young rector was wanted near Boston and in New York, but he declined to be moved so soon. He was wise enough to buckle down to hard study and sermon writing, and soon large audiences began to thrill in response to his mystical insight and prophetic fire. His rare personality was making itself felt on those with whom he came into contact, and they were ready to believe in what he said because they believed in the man. Thus early he gave promise of the popularity of later years.

Throughout the war he was deeply interested in the issues, impatient with the temporizing attitude of the Episcopal General Convention, and sure that the President ought to emancipate the slaves. His brother

George went into the war and died of disease. But conscientiously the Philadelphia rector kept at his parish work, sympathizing with the suffering, cheering the despondent, and instructing from the pulpit and in private conversation those who needed understanding and faith. He was in demand for public address and preached often. He made delightful friendships with other clergymen in his city, enjoying particularly the acquaintance of a representative or two of the Broad Church party in the Church of England.

In the midst of his success as a preacher came an invitation to a professorship in the General Theological School of his church and city. It offered him an opportunity to prove that he had not been mistaken when he thought that he could become a useful teacher. In certain respects he preferred such a position of quiet influence rather than the public character of the ministry. He was ready to accept when his church bestirred itself and his friends began to dissuade him. The church voluntarily offered to lessen his burdens, but urged him to decline the chair. With the best grace he could muster he yielded. But even then influences were at work that were to unseat him. Trinity church in Boston had a fixed purpose to win him back to his native city, and in 1869 it had its way.

Trinity church was not only the leading Episcopal church in Boston, but it was the great church of the diocese. Phillips Brooks was as truly a bishop for the next twenty years as he was during the two years following his election as titular bishop. And his oversight of souls was not limited to those of his own communion.

Protestants of all denominations asked his help. They wrote to him from outside the city, until his desk was piled high with this gratuitous correspondence. Catholics spoke of him as Father Brooks. Aristocrat though he was by birth and education, he forgot all distinctions when he stood face to face with human need. Working men and tired women found comfort and strength in his kindly smile and gentle words and gospel of faith and hope. Children loved him because he loved them. He gave himself unstintedly, and in return the people of Boston and vicinity gave him full measure of affection.

Before Brooks went to Boston he had reached a high point of personal power and popularity; this was by the time he was thirty years old. He reached that age as the war ended, and President Lincoln received his death wound. He went to Harvard College to attend the commemoration service for the men of the University who had laid down their lives for their country. It was a solemn occasion and notable men were in attendance. The Commemoration Ode of James Russell Lowell made the day memorable, but no less so was the prayer of Phillips Brooks. He seemed to sum up all the thoughts and feelings of the people and present them as a holy sacrifice to God. Men remembered that prayer for a lifetime. To Harvard and Boston it was a revelation of a man of God whom from that time they would delight to hear.

A year of travel in Europe followed, a year rich in intellectual and artistic appreciation, a year of physical recuperation from the strain of the period that had

moulded him into full manhood. And what a moulding!
A large, strong physique, an attractive personality, a
powerful intellect, a moral conviction, a spiritual pas-
sion, these were his endowments, fused into a man of
God. Europe only enriched his endowment. He moved
leisurely from Dublin to Jerusalem, spending the last
months of his stay in Switzerland. He reveled in
Jerusalem, he preached in Rome, he hobnobbed with
friends in England, everywhere and with everybody he
was the same happy, companionable friend that he was
at home.

Before he yielded to the Boston call two churches in
San Francisco tried to induce him to come to the
Pacific coast. New York offered him Trinity church
there. The Episcopal Theological Seminary at Cambridge sought him to organize the new school and teach
what he would, but he could hardly accept Cambridge
after he had declined the Philadelphia seminary. He
would have been content to strengthen his preaching
powers and widen the circle of his influence in Philadelphia. That Boston should have succeeded in winning him when the most flattering invitations elsewhere were declined was due, first, to the bonds that
bound him to family and college and native city, and
secondly, to the opportunity to build up a strategic
centre of great influence in the midst of a large student
population and at the heart of New England.

His expectation of wide service was not disappointed.
A new vigour coursed through Trinity parish. Harvard College drafted him regularly as preacher and
spiritual adviser, and he brought a new spiritual tide

into the life of the University. He was in demand for sermons and addresses on special occasions in the country round about. His temper was catholic. So unepiscopal was he in dress and manner, and in his recognition of churches and ministers of other denominations that his subsequent election as bishop was opposed bitterly by high churchmen of his own ecclesiastical body, but his broad-mindedness and consideration made him popular with all denominational groups. Even the Unitarians praised him, and claimed him as one of their own who escaped them, because his family attended Unitarian worship in Boston for a time. It is a significant fact that on the day of his funeral twenty non-Episcopal churches held services of commemoration in his honour.

The life of Brooks bears evidence that the period of bitter denominational rivalry was spent. He represented the nascent idea of a real unity of Christendom, a unity that the Episcopal church has fostered in recent years. Phillips Brooks was one of those great souls who could not be held within the bounds of a particular creed or organization. Loyal to the faith of the Apostles, he was as true an evangelical as a Methodist or Baptist; a believer in the worth and the rights of man, he was as liberal as a Unitarian. He preached to them all, and he took them all into his great heart.

Brooks was a man who could interpret his own times, for he knew men. He could bring a wealth of illustration into his sermons from the past, because he knew history and literature. He could beautify his discourse from sea and sky, because he knew and loved nature. But he was a prophet of the future too, for he had a timeless spirit and a timeless message. Time and space alike were minor items compared with the breadth of sympathy and the sweep of vision of this man of the ages.

The secret of his preaching was his perception of the spiritual values in every man. This was his firm conviction. His responsibility was to awaken the God-consciousness, to move the will to action, to spur on the questioning soul to find God and know Him when he found Him. His *Lectures on Preaching* delivered at Yale in 1877 to the students at the Divinity School, were full of wise suggestions as to method and content, but the theme that spoke with steady rhythm through the whole was the minister's mission to awaken the soul to a consciousness of God and eternal life. His was a pure soul, a holy life lived in that awareness of the Eternal. And the man himself shone through the sentences that he wrote, for the lectures were the story of his own soul. Somehow he knew that truth means little in the abstract, but must pass through the medium of personality. The Lectures became a classic on preaching from the hour of their delivery.

The Yale Lectures were followed shortly by another series of lectures resulting in a book on the *Influence of Jesus*. He preached the sermon at the Massachusetts convention of the church and at Harvard in the same year. The next summer he was in England, and preached by request to Queen Victoria in the royal chapel at Windsor. During that same year he might have become the head of the University of Pennsylvania. In 1881 he was asked to accept the position of preacher to Harvard College and professor of Christian ethics. All these are evidences of his ability and his popularity. But the pulpit of Trinity church was his throne and professorial chair, and his purpose to remain in Boston could not be shaken. The old building in which the church worshipped had gone down in the great fire that swept the city in 1872, and in the new Back Bay a new structure was built in the central location of Copley Square, where the St. Gaudens statue of Phillips Brooks stands to-day by the side of the crowded way.

In 1882 he had another year abroad and he extended his journeying as far as India. He was showered with invitations of all sorts, a recognition of his worth even on the other side of the world. A second volume of his sermons appeared about the same time. On his return to America he plunged into discussions of the subjects that were absorbing the attention of church people. The decade of the eighties echoed with the strife of minds agnostic and skeptical of the old theology in the light of new knowledge of the universe. Phillips Brooks read thoughtfully, but preserved his sanity and careful judgment. Welcoming much of the new, he would not lose his hold on the central truth of loyalty to Jesus Christ as the dependable teacher of spiritual truth. Other tenets are on the circumference of theology. He championed the right to think freely, but not to think irresponsibly.

In 1885 Oxford University honoured Brooks with the degree of doctor of divinity on one of his visits to England. As he came to the half century milestone in his life it was evident that he was ripening to an even richer fulness of manhood. It was realized that he had the capacity to serve the Church in the most honourable positions it had to give. The assistant bishopric of Pennsylvania was offered to him in 1886, but he did not welcome it. He was a modest man and well content with his pastorate. In 1891 the last great honour came to him in his election as Bishop of Massachusetts. That office he could not refuse. Phillips Brooks was not without honour in his city and country. Newspapers vied with his friends in recommending his election, and when it was confirmed by the denomination at large there was great rejoicing even though his local church and public men of Boston realized the loss that it meant to Trinity and to the city.

Phillips Brooks was faithful to his obligations as a superintendent. He wore himself out in his official visitations. Before the first month of 1893 his health gave way and he sank into his grave. Men could not think of him as dead, only translated to a larger sphere of usefulness. On a tablet in Phillips Brooks House, Harvard, the centre of religious activities in the University, they inscribed their estimate of him in the words: " A preacher of righteousness and hope, majestic in stature, impetuous in utterance, rejoicing in the truth, unhampered by bonds of church or station, he brought by his life and doctrine fresh faith to a people, fresh meaning to ancient creeds; to this University he gave constant love, large service, high example."

20

WALTER RAUSCHENBUSCH

THE growth of cities as throbbing centres of human industry is as characteristic of the twentieth century as rural life was character- istic of the nineteenth. In its raw, crude youth the industrial town is guilty of cruelty and greed, and those who are least fit to fight the battle for existence and profit suffer in misery and squalor. Social prob- lems bristle in such communities, and the cry of the wretched echoes to the skies, " Lord, how long? "

The makers of modern Christianity have been for the most part country-born, but the city has given birth to one and another who have voiced its sorrows and condemned its greed. Walter Rauschenbusch was one of these. If Phillips Brooks had a message to the cul- tured of Philadelphia and Boston to look tolerantly upon one another's beliefs and to find a common ground for their faith, Walter Rauschenbusch had a prophet's message of intolerance for social sin and a challenge to those who have wealth and power to use their assets as held in trust for the common weal. Rauschenbusch will be remembered in Christian his- tory as the apostle of a social gospel, an interpreter of Jesus as the builder of a better social order, a teacher and preacher of social righteousness.

Like Brooks Rauschenbusch was born in the city. Rochester was the home of his father, who had emigrated from Germany in the disturbed decade of the forties that he might find freedom of thought and utterance in America, and had found his opportunity to speak and to teach in the German theological school in Rochester. Walter was of clerical lineage. Seven generations had produced preachers. He had a good heritage to start with, and when he came to consciousness on October 4, 1861, he was in an environment that promised him many advantages. As a boy he did not have to toil on the farm like Bushnell, or hire himself out for employment like Moody. He went through the course of public schooling that the city provided, and found his way to the University of Rochester where he was graduated in the class of 1884.

From childhood he was a real democrat. The spirit of the father was reborn in the son. He too must think and speak without restraint, and what he asked for himself he asked for others. His human sympathy sent him into the ministry after a theological course at Rochester Theological Seminary, which he completed in 1886. Then because he was a friend of the poor he went to New York City and accepted the pastorate of the Second German Baptist church of the metropolis at a salary of six hundred dollars. There for eleven years he toiled without thought of self, preaching the gospel of good will and living it with a consecration of soul and body to those who had need. He never spared himself. Day and night he was at the service of all who had need of him. He was a living example of those who minister to their Lord in serving the sick and miserable, the poor and naked. Because he thought not of his own health, he lost his hearing through untimely exposure after a severe illness, and he carried that handicap to the grave.   In spite of it he was cheerful and happy, and now and again he tapped a vein of humour or of poetry that delighted his friends.

Many times his own heart was scorched by the evils that he saw and felt.   He suffered with others.   The sordid side of city life was uppermost.   He felt how unchristian is modern civilization, and he longed to help remould it into the kingdom of God.   He knew that the true principle of life was service, but he knew that the commonwealth of God would be a long time coming if it waited for every man to be converted from profit-making to service-giving.   He saw that individual religion must be supplemented by social religion, that the institutions that make up society must be reformed and readjusted if the world is to become better.   That meant that modern industry must be purified of its selfishness, modern government must be redirected to serve the interests of all the people, and the modern Church must realize that it is the guardian of the people's weal.

In the year 1893 he helped to organize a group of kindred spirits into the Brotherhood of the Kingdom. The purpose was to encourage one another to stand manfully for a social Christianity, and to propagate the idea as widely as possible.   It was not at that time a popular or well-understood idea.   The churches were absorbed in their material interests or in evangelistic efforts at home and abroad.   The new social science was only just beginning to draw to itself some of the attention and interest that had been given lavishly to natural science. Men were in business and politics for what they could get out of them. It was a time of business depression, when those in contact with working people were keenly aware of the misfortune of unemployment, of the hard fate of the poor, and of the mass of human misery in the slums of the city. The heart of Walter Rauschenbusch bled more than once as he moved among them.

He toiled through the period of distress until prosperity came again, and when his alma mater invited him to return to the Seminary as professor, he saw his opportunity to impress his thoughts and experiences on young men who were giving their lives to Christian service, and he responded favourably. He might have felt that he had served his apprenticeship with the poor and now he might forget them, but that was not his way. Into his teaching of history he poured his soul. He made the past live again by linking it with the present. And when it was possible to point out the social application of historical principles, he urged his pupils to read history in the light of the present as well as the present in the light of the past.

As a teacher he had the confidence of his pupils in his intellectual equipment and he stirred their interest, but more than that they loved him for his kindly spirit. With clearness and earnestness he pressed home the day's lesson, and succeeded in leaving with students his convictions and point of view, even when they lost the specific factors that entered into the

story.   His classroom was not a place of drudgery but
of inspiration.   As a friend he reached out to men
and women in all the earth.   He felt kinship of spirit
with all who were working for human betterment, the
settlement workers, the writers and speakers on reform,
the teachers and ministers of all schools and com-
munions.   It mattered little to him how much or little
a person had of mental equipment or attainment, if his
moral energy and intelligence were enlisted in the service of mankind.   And all sorts and conditions of men
learned to love and trust him.

Rauschenbusch was known to a relatively small
circle until the publication of his book, *Christianity
and the Social Crisis,* in 1907.   It was an opportune
time for his message.   The social mind was sur-
charged with a growing conviction that there was a
social crisis.   Rauschenbusch clarified that mind as
Luther did with his Ninety-five Theses in 1517.   For
a long time he had known that he wanted to put his
message into a book.   There were other books on conventional lines that he was interested to write also, but
this subject was near his heart.   He began it in the
summer vacation, and then had to lay it aside.   A
second period of application brought it to completion.
Then he went abroad for a year's study.   When he
returned he was a marked man.   The book met criticism from those who were jealous for personal religion
in its accepted forms, but it came as a revelation to
many Christians, opening a door to a larger field of
opportunity and obligation.   To those who were out
of sympathy with religion it seemed unpractical when

it advocated Christianity as the remedy for social ills, but a growing body of loyal friends acknowledged Rauschenbusch as the prophet of social reform that the times needed. " People told me," said the author, " that it gave them a new experience of religion and a new feeling about Christ."

The book made its way everywhere. It was read on the train as well as in the study, talked about wherever in conversation the theme of discussion chanced upon social reform. It was translated abroad, even to Japan. It suggested other treatises on the same subject until a flood of literature poured from the presses. Ministers discussed it in their clubs and conferences, and preached its doctrines from their pulpits. Workingmen pored over it, and while some scoffed, others felt that he spoke what was in their hearts.

Immediately he was besieged with requests to speak from the public platform, and he responded as often as he could feel justified in being away from his main task of teaching. In the years that followed he visited colleges and seminaries, lecturing on various foundations. He did not forget how to preach; once he was the preacher at the annual convention of the Northern Baptists to which he belonged. He had the satisfaction of working with other men of his own kind within denominational lines. But he took peculiar pleasure in speaking to working people on those issues that commanded his allegiance, never forgetting to urge the Christian principles that must underlie the solution of all social problems.

Within a few years after the publication of his book

the open forum movement was launched, and on its platforms he found his freest opportunity. No speaker was more popular than he. At the Ford Hall forum in Boston long lines of people waited in the street until the doors were opened that they might not fail of admittance. Smaller communities organized similarly for the discussion of social questions in which the people were interested. Industrial relations were especially popular, and along with these civic matters and international affairs. A reputable speaker with a real message and then a period of questions from the floor answered by the speaker was the method of the forum, and the give and take of the period of questioning was enjoyed by the eager audience. The keenest minds on both sides were brought into play, and a real battle of wits ensued. In general the meetings furnished a genuine attempt to understand and interpret the issues under review, and oftentimes a deeply religious spirit pervaded the gathering. That was always true when Rauschenbusch was the speaker, because with him all social questions were moral questions, and human welfare was an important part of his religion.

Rauschenbusch was cheered greatly by the evidences that were apparent within a few years that the churches were awakening to their social responsibility. The social changes that were taking place with the rapid growth of the cities and the incoming of foreigners compelled the churches to socialize their religious thinking. The churches had looked upon the foreigner as a problem in religion. If he was a

Catholic he might be a danger to Protestantism. If
he was a Protestant he should be brought into membership in American churches. City and home mission
societies had been working on the religious problem.
But now immigration was seen as a social problem,
and the alien was looked upon as a man with social
needs as well as a possible proselyte. Institutional
churches were established in the downtown sections
of the cities, and their programs included ministry to
body and mind as well as spirit.

Another social problem was the depletion of rural
areas of country by city-ward migration. The Young
Men's Christian Association and the Young Women's
Christian Association had been in existence for a half
century with the purpose of keeping in touch with
young people who had come from country homes to
new occupations in the cities. But now the problem
of the country districts faced the denominations as
rural churches decayed and died, and it was seen to
be only another phase of the one persistent problem
of social adjustments.

Other evidences multiplied that the churches were
becoming conscious that they had a social responsibility as churches. Their members had been active
as individuals in all forms of philanthropy, but great
movements were on foot with which the Church as
an institution was concerned vitally, and towards
which it ought to take a definite attitude of active
friendship or criticism. Labour had become clamor-
ous for its rights. Socialism enlisted increasing numbers of workers and their sympathizers in a program

to set right social inequalities by bringing in a new social order. More ministers than formerly, with their natural sympathy for the oppressed, were preaching and writing on themes of social Christianity. In England and America a literature of social Christianity was coming into existence with special stress on the social teachings of Jesus and the application of Christianity to present-day life. The new social life was different from the earlier humanitarianism in that it went to the roots of social evils, and the talk of the time was about reconstruction of the social order as much as about remedies and relief in the present order. Social service was a phrase constantly upon the lips, and all sorts of methods were tried.

By the first years of the twentieth century a number of the religious denominations in the United States had organized social service commissions through the initiative of a few who were most interested, and these commissions through printed literature and reports of conferences were attempting to get the ear of the churches and to diffuse social intelligence. In 1912 the Federal Council of Churches of Christ in America adopted a social creed for the churches.

Rauschenbusch was enthusiastic over the increasing realization of social obligation, and he expressed his feelings in a second book entitled *Christianizing the Social Order*. In it he pointed out the gains that had been made within a few years and the changes that were taking place in the social situation, with a renewed emphasis on the duty of Christian people to carry religion into all the social relations. The new

book met with a cordial response from those who had
come to look to Rauschenbusch for leadership in the
campaign to socialize organized Christianity and to
christianize society.

There were two divergent tendencies in the ranks of
those who were concerned with human welfare.   A
large majority of church people believed that such
welfare depended on personal religion, and they could
not see that the application of religion to social institutions like business and industry was the business
of the churches.   It was mainly for such people that
Rauschenbusch wrote his first two books.   The other
tendency was that of persons who could see no value
in religion or the Church except as they helped on
the social movement.   For them he spoke in the forums.   He wanted as far as possible to give a religious
tone to the forums.   A few forum leaders opened the
forum meetings with prayer, but few prayers had a
social content. Church prayer-books contained no pro-
vision for such occasions as forums.   Rauschenbusch
went to work to prepare such a manual.   The result
was his *Prayers of the Social Awakening*.   With a
surge of deep feeling he expressed his hope and faith
for a better day, and in many gatherings of people in-
articulate longing and conviction found new and vivid
expression in words of power and beauty.

The social awakening in religion resulted in a re-
consideration of certain religious conceptions.   One
was as to the meaning of righteousness.   Virtue was
supposed to have benevolence as its motive, but it consisted in such personal excellences as truthfulness,

purity, and the like.   The new social teaching was that
ethical conduct between groups was an essential to
righteousness, and that it was more important for an
employer to treat a worker humanely than to be a good
provider for his family or a consistent Sunday worship-
per in the church.   Another conception was as to the
meaning of salvation.   The stress of evangelism was
upon the necessity of individual regeneration for the
sake of eternal happiness in another world.   The new
thought was that heaven begins here on earth and that
individual salvation is incomplete without social salvation.   Social institutions needed conversion.   Social
ideals needed reshaping.   The idea of the kingdom of
God needed redefinition.

Considerations such as these sent Rauschenbusch on
a quest for a theology to match the social gospel.   He
had already published a small handbook on the social
principles of Jesus.   Other men had offered suggestions for an improved theology, but no one had re-
shaped the Christian system of thought from the social
point of view.   With characteristic modesty Rauschenbusch felt that he could do no more than pioneer in
this field, but he would do what he could.   The result
was his *A Theology for the Social Gospel,* issued in
1917.   It was an attempt to make plain the implica-
tions of the gospel of Jesus, and to relate the best of
Christian thought to the twentieth century.   It made
no effort to be complete.   Rauschenbusch knew that
the time was hardly ripe for that, but he believed that
the book " had to be written sometime," and he must
make his contribution while he could, for the sake of

young men who were trying to relate the new emphasis
to the old and for the sake of older men whose eyes
were opening to new visions of truth. The book was
welcomed by those who had felt the tonic of the new
thought, and helped to increase the admiration of
those who had thought of him as a prophet rather than
a constructive theologian.

With the publication of his *Theology* the active contributions of Walter Rauschenbusch to the social revival were nearly over. His sensitive heart had
grieved over the World War and its bitterness. His
health was breaking, though his friends hoped that it
was only a temporary interruption to his work. But
with the end of the war came the end of his life on
the twenty-fifth of July, 1918. The *Congregationalist*
in its issue of the eighth of August expressed the feeling of all who knew him when it said: " Professor
Rauschenbusch by his untiring industry, his comprehensive visions of the kingdom of God, and his em-
bodiment of the finest human qualities, earned a commanding place among American religious leaders. His
death at fifty-seven, after a long and severe illness,
comes all too soon from our limited point of view, con-
sidering the need of such men as he in the reconstruction of our disordered and war-stricken world. Yet he
has made remarkable and enduring contributions to
Christian thought and has helped to shape the plan of
campaign for many an intrepid soldier of Jesus Christ."

21

BORDEN PARKER BOWNE

IN a different department of thought where speculative minds puzzle out the problems of existence another teacher made his mark in the last part of the nineteenth century. Borden Parker Bowne was a descendant of Puritan ancestors, who came to Salem early in colonial days. Some of the family went later to New Jersey, and there the future philosopher was born in 1847. His father was one of not a few men at that time who mingled trades and professions. He made his living from agriculture, but as a justice of the peace and an occasional preacher of religion he added to his acquaintance and his influence with others. He was an unswerving opponent of the liquor traffic and of slavery at a time when most people were willing to compromise with both.

The son inherited a liking for books, and grew up with a shy disposition and a fondness for thinking things over by himself. Partly by a course of instruction in Pennington Seminary, partly by his own study, he was prepared for the sophomore class in New York University, and there he reached a pinnacle of reputation for brilliant scholarship that had never been surpassed. He was graduated valedictorian of his class in 1871. For a year he taught school, an apprenticeship to a life task which so many have tried before they have fairly found themselves. Then, with an in-

242

terest in religion that vied with philosophy for ascendancy in his mind, he became pastor of a Methodist
church in Whitestone, New York. A period of study
in Europe followed at the German universities of Halle
and Goettingen. There in the midst of German
thought he probed further into the problems of the
mind, but his future profession was not yet determined.
On his return to America in 1875 he became assistant
professor of modern languages in the University of the
City of New York for a year, and simultaneously was
religious editor of the *New York Independent*.

Bowne's keen, logical mind fitted him for the legal
profession, and some of his friends urged him to equip
himself for the law, but his tastes were not sympathetic with such a profession. While he was an undergraduate he made a critical study of the philosophy of
Herbert Spencer, which was commanding the attention
of all scholarly minds. The results of his study were
published as an article in the *New Englander*. The
article was unsigned and was thought by most readers
to have been written by a mature scholar. In his own
circle Bowne's reputation was enhanced by it. The
year after he returned from abroad, while he was teaching and writing in New York, his own Methodist denomination drafted him for its new university in Boston. He was asked to become the head of the department of philosophy. This opportunity was much to
his liking and from that time he identified himself
with Boston University, turning a deaf ear to all the
flattering invitations that came to him from other universities. His service as professor and dean of the

graduate school brought increasing fame to the university over a period of nearly thirty-five years.

Boston University was the training school for the Methodist youth of New England north of Connecticut, and for theological students whom the city and the university attracted from all over the country. Bowne had an opportunity to stamp the impress of his mind upon a whole generation of leaders in the churches, both clerical and lay. His responsibility was profound. It was a time when science and philosophy both were tending to discredit the tenets of evangelical Christianity, when it would be easy to create an agnostic attitude of mind in the student body, and a spirit of disunity and criticism in the faculties of the college and the theological school. On the other hand, the professor of philosophy might have taken an obscurantist attitude towards all modern thought, and so have lost the confidence of open-minded students in the professor, the university, and the church.

From the beginning he made philosophy interesting. He had a way of presenting it in concrete pictures so that the eye of an undergraduate might visualize it. He had an original way of putting things, lecturing briskly, often humorously, permitting relevant questions but impatient with lazy and prejudiced minds, allowing plenty of occasion for discussion, but never wasting time. When he had examined the subject thoroughly, he left it for appropriation to the individual student, expecting him to assimilate it, and then describe his mental reactions at the next class quiz.

Bowne's mind was honest and critical. He would

not reject a conclusion because it did not agree with an opinion that he had formed or with a scheme of thought that he had accepted. But certain spiritual convictions were rooted in him, and these served as an anchor to his faith while he probed here and there into the sea of knowledge and opinion. He could not doubt the existence of God, whether as First Cause of creation or brooding Providence, but the nature of God and the method of His revelation to man were open questions for the play of reason and insight. He did not doubt the immortality of the soul, but he could and did investigate the psychic nature and learn how it works. He looked upon philosophy and theology as distinct, yet he knew that they must be in harmony. Theology depends on faith aided by reason, philosophy on reason plus insight and faith.

The Boston professor was not satisfied to scratch the surface of philosophy or to confine himself to one department of it. He was teaching it from all sides, and his thinking took a wide range. He made it his business to clarify one after another of the problems that beset the student. Since the problem of knowledge is fundamental to all sound thinking, he faced the question whether man acquires knowledge through his sense perceptions of a material world, or through the intellectual processes of a mind that is capable of rationalizing. That had been a mooted question for centuries, but natural science had tipped the scales in favour of the scientific method of getting at facts by observation and investigation and then generalizing on the basis of the facts.

The second problem that he faced was the problem of reality. Once possessed of the tools of knowledge, the next job of the philosopher is to find whether mind or matter is the ultimate reality. Is nature, the material things we can see and feel and hear, the sum and end of all things? Or is there a spirit back of it all akin to the inner spirit of man that permeates all and outlasts all, the unseen background of the visible universe? After the discoveries of scientists like Darwin and the philosophizing of men like Herbert Spencer and Huxley, it seemed to many that at best it was impossible to know anything beyond. Yet Fiske, the interpreter of Spencer to America, pointed from nature to God.

The third problem in philosophy was the problem of ethics. What are the grounds of obligation, and is the moral imperative whose voice a man hears within himself anything more than the voice of social custom that has come to him with the approval of the past stamped upon the soul? What is the end of life? Is it to enjoy as much as possible, forgetting obligation to God or man, or is it to follow the gleam of purity and righteousness whenever it beckons as an ideal?

It was not for most men—teachers, evangelists, pastors, social workers—to bother with these problems. They had neither the ability nor the time. But they are everybody's concern when they are translated from the unknown language of philosophy to the pulpit and the teacher's desk, to the printed page, and even to the seamy side of social living in the workaday world. What a man thinks affects his conduct profoundly.

And so Borden P. Bowne in his classroom on Beacon Hill in Boston was fashioning souls no less truly than Moody in the pulpit or Rauschenbusch on the platform of the open forum.

Bowne was dependable as a teacher because he had a firm grasp on the basic problems of philosophy. He thought his way through to definite conclusions. He knew the findings of the scientist and the speculations of the philosopher. He never forgot that every truth must be seen in relation to the whole, and he was fond of setting a task for his pupils in some other department of thought that might throw a sidelight on the subject in hand. For the benefit of pupils and former students he put his principal conclusions into systematic form for the press, until in the course of years he had mapped out with fair completeness the whole field of philosophy.

The substance of his thought was that man is a free moral being who has to learn from experience both truth and wisdom. Knowledge and reality are of the inner consciousness, substantiated by the things of sense. To believe that man is only a complex machine or a puppet to be pulled about by invisible springs was so contrary to his inner experience that it was unthinkable as a working proposition of life, and that was the true test as he saw it. Back of all the things that please or worry us is first the personal self, and then the personal God. The thought of personality stands out clearly in all Bowne's thinking, and it was appropriate that he should call his philosophy Personalism. And as the personal element is at the heart of religion, his religion and philosophy could not be far apart. That was what made him so helpful an interpreter to the developing minds of theological students who thronged his classes. He showed them how they could be critical in their studies, and yet positive in their convictions. He was impatient of obstructions sometimes put in the way of free thinking by certain prejudiced men in the ministry of his own church, men who persecuted him until it was apparent that a teacher with the saintly soul of Bowne could never be convicted of heresy in an ecclesiastical court. He was not very liberal in his theology. He believed in Christ as a Saviour from sin and he saw no panacea for ignorance in any of the modern discoveries, but he championed the right to think and was scathing in his criticism of those who would shut the door. When he had completed his published survey of philosophy, he turned his attention to clearing up some of the theological difficulties that were troubling students of religion. In such books as his *Studies of Christianity* he freed certain doctrines from their ancient setting, and gave them a clear, original interpretation. Never disciplined by the routine of the theological seminary, he was deeply religious, and he was familiar with the Bible from childhood. His primary aim was to hew a straight path through the maze of human opinion to the thought of God Himself, and he cared not what he must cut away if only he could let in the light.

So from his throne in the classroom Bowne mastered the minds of his pupils not by any external authority, but by the reasonableness of his exposition and the kindly winsomeness of his personal friendship. For the teacher was a friend to every inquiring mind. He was worth listening to because he saw all life and thought in the light of eternity. He was not oblivious to the surge of world affairs. He delighted to draw out in conversation the opinions of others on international questions, and he had his own contribution to make. He journeyed once around the world, receiving the plaudits of those who liked his books, and of some men in the Far East who had sat under his instruction in America. He prized the opportunity to test his opinions of world conditions by evidence at first hand.

A philosopher to some people seems hardly human, but that could not be true of Bowne. His university contacts, especially with young people, would have prevented that. He had warm friends who loved as well as admired him, but the pressure of university duties together with his writing prevented extending his acquaintance as far as he would have liked. He was fond of throwing aside the philosopher's cloak to work in his garden, and it was his cherished wish that he might live long enough to get a closer acquaintance with nature. He passed on, as nature was telling anew the old, old story of resurrection, on the first day of April, 1910.

Borden Parker Bowne was an exponent of the best Christian thinking that the present age has produced. Trained in the Wesleyan school of religious thought in his youth, growing to maturity at a time when all opinion was brought to the test of science, teaching in a city which had been the centre of Unitarianism from its organization, ranging fearlessly in his thought to the very bounds of the universe, yet keeping his simple faith in the realities of spiritual experience, he was an example to the men who were going out from university halls year after year to the leadership of the churches. He could not be stampeded by new discoveries or held back by ancient barriers in his march forward. With the windows of his mind open to all the breezes that blew there were no cobwebbed chambers in it, but he could not be swept off his feet by gales of criticism. His own radiant personality reflected the God whom he knew by reason and experience. Moulded by the spirit of God into His likeness, he was fitted to be a maker of modern religion for those who think.

The Christianity of to-day is not the product of a few minds thinking their thoughts through a few centuries and a few active leaders working vigorously for the coming of a divine kingdom among men. It is the consequence of the thought and activity of unnumbered multitudes of men and women who have lived from the dawn of history until now. But the last seven centuries have brought a better understanding of the real essence of religion, a clearer interpretation of the message that Jesus came to give. And among the many who have lived and taught along the highway of history a few have left an abiding influence, especially among the people of the churches. They are the pathfinders for the pilgrims who are on the march to the Eternal. • They are those who have carried the torch that others might follow the gleam.

Francis of Assisi was born into an age that was under the authority of an historic church. He did not revolt from it, but he taught it the meaning of service and democracy. John Wyclif a hundred and fifty years later reacted farther from the institutional religion of Rome, denied the sanctity of the priest or the Mass as God's avenue of approach to man, and turned the attention of the people of his time to the teachings of the Bible. Martin Luther, when the people of the Fatherland were reading earnestly the story of the gospels and questioning the guidance of the old Church, dared to affirm that the inner attitude of the individual soul was more important for salvation than anything that the Church could do. He could not free himself entirely from the training that he had received, but he could champion the right to think for himself against all the threats of Church and state. John Calvin stressed the absolute dependence of the individual on God and His sovereign will, and the impossibility of escape from personal responsibility to God. Both Luther and Calvin maintained the close union of Church and State. Luther thought that the State must decide the forms of religion, and Calvin that the Church must dictate to the State what its action should be with reference to morals and religion. They won freedom from Rome, but not from external control of religion.

Religious liberty was the contribution of Robert Browne and Roger Williams and George Fox. Browne broke away from church establishment in England and declared the principles of Congregationalism as an independent method of church organization. Williams denied the right of any body of men to dictate the religion of an individual, and ventured to found a colony on the principle of the absolute separation of Church and State, and the right to freedom to think and speak on the subject of religion. Fox went so far in his reaction to the authority of the external as to abolish all sacraments except the inner cleansing and fellowship of the soul of man through his contacts with God in silent worship.

Puritanism in its various forms had freed religion from many of its old encumbrances, but it had not made it vital and personal for the common people. The evangelism of Edwards and Wesley accomplished that great purpose in England and America. Asbury carried Wesley's practical gospel to the far-flung frontiers of expanding America. Oberlin was content to serve his rural parish in the mountains of the old French frontier. Carey projected his soul into the broad wastes of eastern heathenism. All these illustrated how far was the reach and how broad the application of the Gospel of Jesus.

But Protestantism became dogmatic and sectarian in America. It needed the simplification of the creeds by Campbell, the liberalizing of thought and the dignifying of humanity by Channing, the emphasis of Horace Bushnell upon the kindlier aspects of a loving Father and His gentle leading of the mind even of a little child. Moody was a reminder that Christian nurture does not do away with the necessity of evangelistic preaching to those who have sinned, and the response that he gained both in Great Britain and America proved that man is incurably religious in his convictions and the deeper aspirations of his life. Drummond reconciled science and religion and demonstrated that it was the same God who made nature and the heart of man. Brooks pleaded for a wider catholicity among Christians of every name, and lived out the simple religion of Jesus in the centre of American culture. Rauschenbusch felt the hurt of the masses who toil and with eager voice and passionate pen interpreted Jesus anew as the Saviour of human society. And Borden Parker Bowne took the lore of the ages and reviewed it in the crucible of his own thought, took the tradition of the Church and made it glow in the light of reason and personal experience, took the wisdom of the present and made it luminous with the light of eternity, and left as his legacy the confident assurance that God is back of all to will and to work according to His good pleasure, offering to every one who will the privilege of being co-workers with Him for the better age that yet shall be.

History is not a record of man's failure to make good in the world where God has placed him. He falls to rise again, errs to think more wisely, strives and wins and strives again, but with the divine urge within him and the Cross to inspire him, he presses on his way for the prize that is set before him, the possibility of a home in the presence of God wherein dwell righteousness and peace and eternal satisfaction.